INDIAN IVORIES FROM AFGHANISTAN
THE BEGRAM HOARD

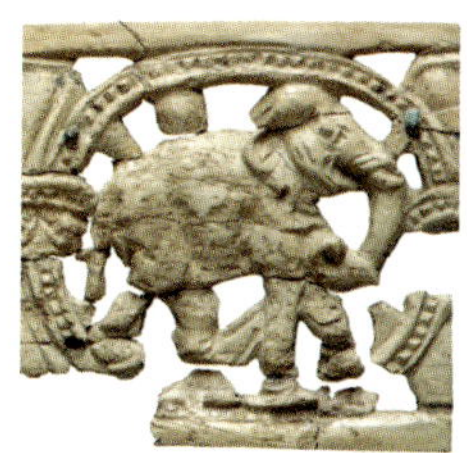

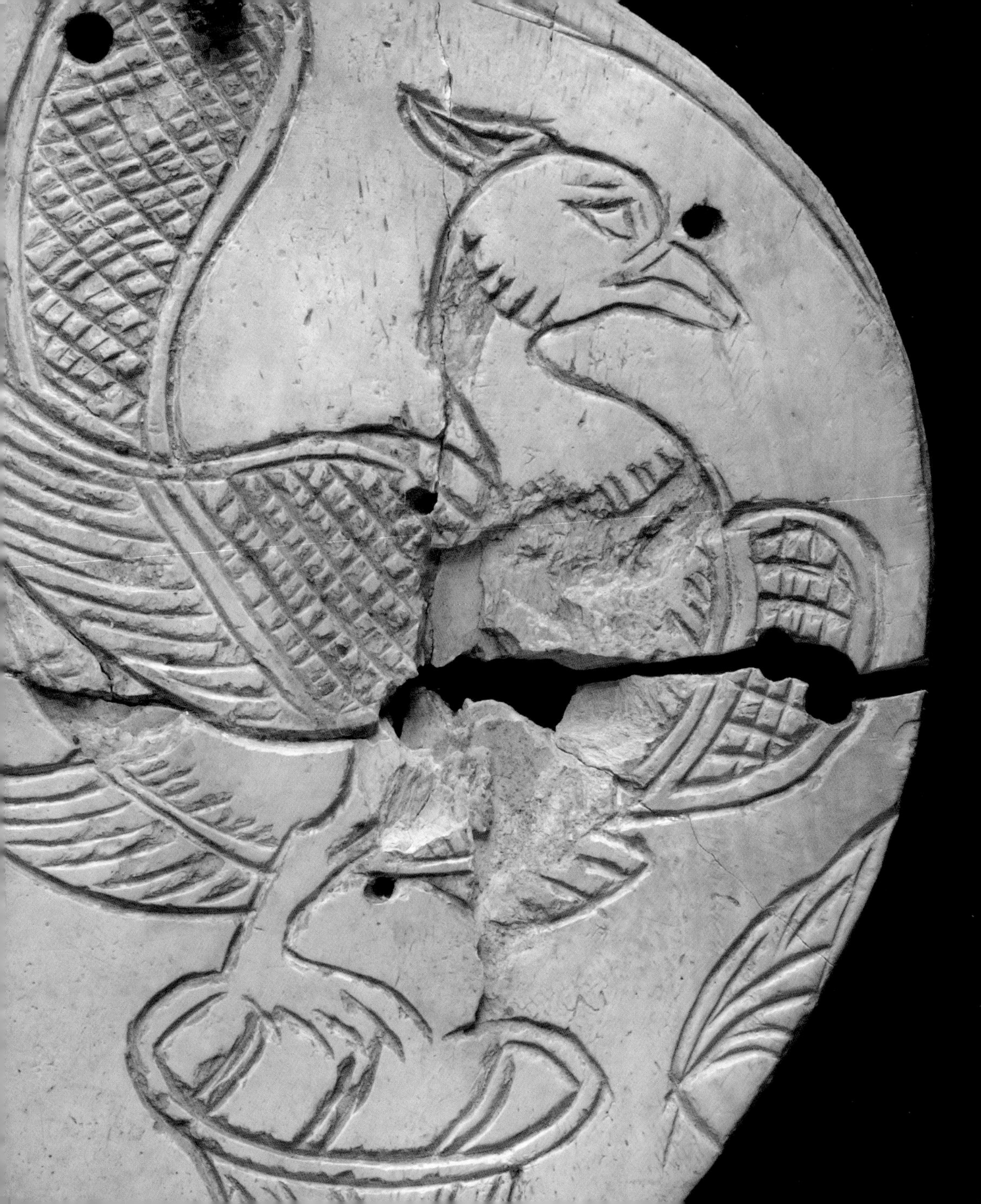

THE BEGRAM HOARD

ST JOHN SIMPSON

THE BRITISH MUSEUM PRESS

This book is published to accompany an exhibition
at the British Museum, 3 March – 3 July 2011
Published in 2011 by the British Museum Press
A division of the British Museum Company Ltd
38 Russell Square
London WC1B 3QQ
www.britishmuseum.org

This exhibition has been made possible with the
assistance of the Government Indemnity Scheme which
is provided by the Department for Culture, Media and
Sport and administered by the Museums, Libraries and
Archives Council.

The conservation of the objects has been made possible
by funding from the Bank of America Merrill Lynch Art
Conservation Programme.

A catalogue record for this book is available from the
British Library
ISBN 978-0-7141-1178-0
Design by Price Watkins
Printed in Spain

The papers used in this book are natural, renewable and
recyclable products and the manufacturing processes are
expected to conform to the environmental regulations of
the country of origin.

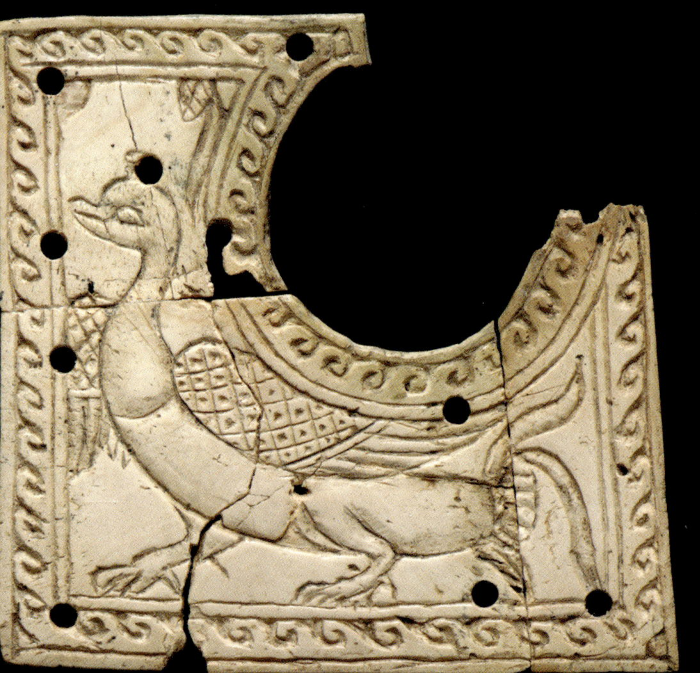

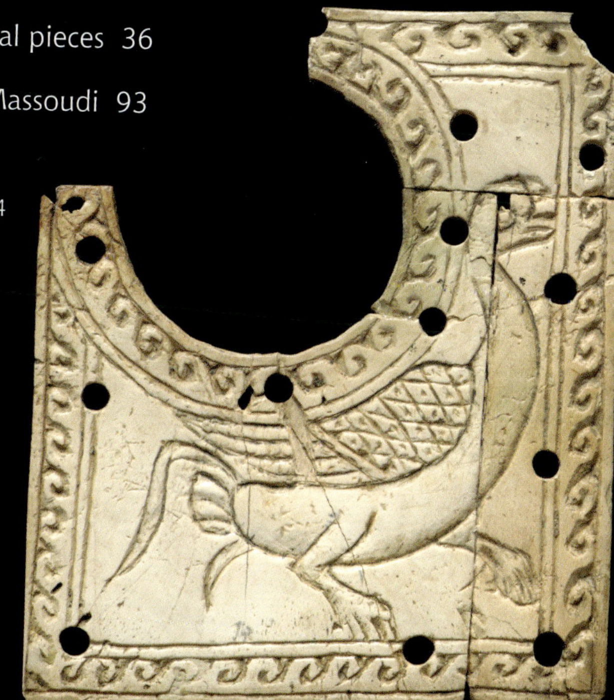

Introduction

by Neil MacGregor, Director of the British Museum

THE INLAYS from Begram are among the great treasures divided between the National Museum in Afghanistan and the Musée Guimet in Paris. Discovered in the 1930s by archaeologists from the Délégation Archéologique Française en Afghanistan excavating in the ancient Kushan summer capital of Kapisa at Begram, they vividly illustrate the desire for comfortable living and luxury trade in the first or early second century AD. They were originally attached to wooden sofas and foot stools made in India and were resplendent in full colour. They are also very rare, as ivory is highly fragile.

The story of these pieces is particularly compelling. They were found in very poor condition, excavated under difficult circumstances and many were posthumously published as the excavators were killed during the Second World War.

The pieces belonging to Kabul were exhibited there until political events forced the closure of the National Museum in 1978. Over the next twenty-five years, their fate remained uncertain. Some of the

finest pieces were revealed in 2004, restored and put on travelling
exhibition but the whereabouts of others remained undisclosed.
It later transpired that they had been exported and sold illicitly on
the black market in antiquities. Thanks to a great act of generosity,
they will now return to Kabul. We are delighted to announce the
recovery of this group of twenty pieces, including some of the most
exquisite from Begram, which have been re-conserved and are now
ready for repatriation to Afghanistan.

We are very grateful to those brave Afghans who have worked
tirelessly to preserve their culture, and it has been a great privilege
to be a small part of the recovery and return of pieces belonging to
the National Museum of Afghanistan. We look forward to the display
of these lovely pieces in Kabul in the near future where they will again
underline the close relationship that Afghanistan has always had with
its neighbours.

1

The discovery of Begram

IN JULY 1833 the English explorer Charles Masson (1800–53) discovered the ancient city of Begram, some eighty kilometres north of Kabul and commanding a strategic pair of mountain passes through the Hindu Kush that connect Bactria with northern Pakistan. He collected a huge number of coins and minor antiquities from the area, many later acquired by the British Museum. He proposed that he had discovered Alexandria ad Caucasum, one of the cities founded by Alexander the Great (356–323 BC), although the earliest objects he collected were from *c.* 200 BC and later pieces range up to the thirteenth century.

Archaeological excavations were finally undertaken a century later. In September 1922 Alfred Foucher, acting for the French, signed a treaty with the Afghan government in Kabul. This gave French archaeologists a virtual monopoly on archaeological research and gave diplomatic status to the newly created Délégation Archéologique Française en Afghanistan. In the following year

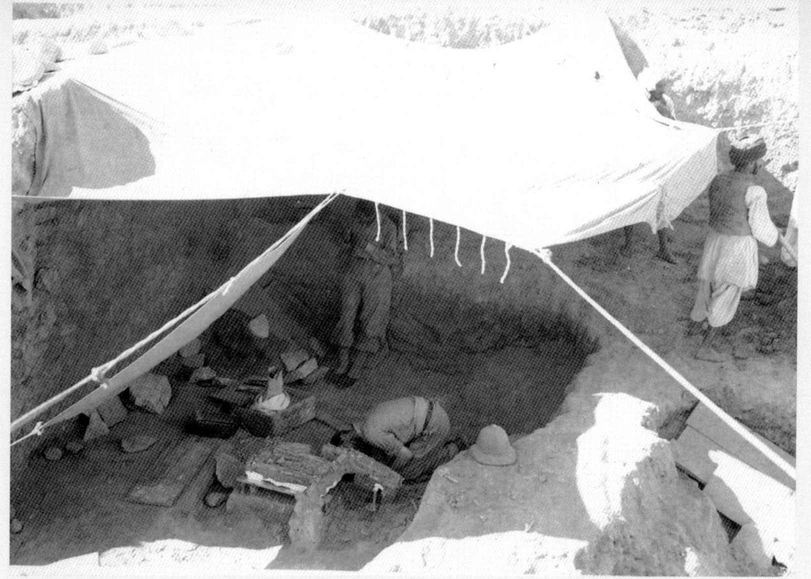

Views of excavations in progress at Begram and illustrating the fragile state of the ivories at the moment of discovery. A tented awning was stretched over the excavation yet at times the internal temperature still reached 45°C.

André Godard, then Director General of the Archaeological Service of Iran, was appointed its first director of excavations. The principal focus was art-historical and on sites which could provide information on the eastward diffusion of Hellenism, the origin of Gandharan art and its relation to Buddhist art, and the extent of Silk Road trade through Afghanistan. Several sites were promptly investigated, including Begram.

This city site was re-identified by Foucher as ancient Kapisa, the summer capital and residence of the Kushan kings whose powerful state stretched from northern Afghanistan to northern India between the first and fourth centuries AD. Excavations were begun by Jean Carl and Jacques Meunié in 1936 and continued by Meunié with Joseph and Ria Hackin until

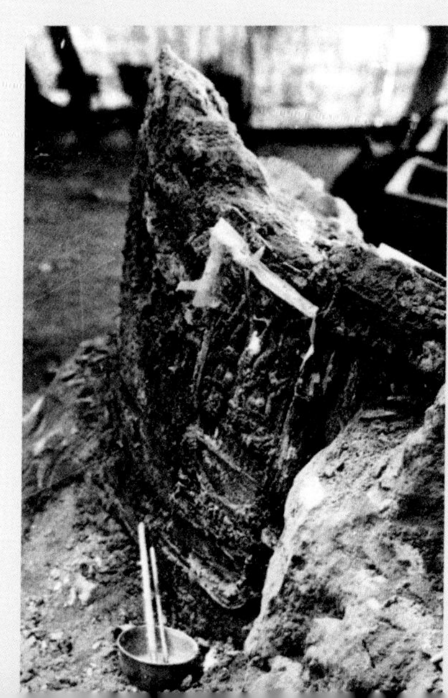

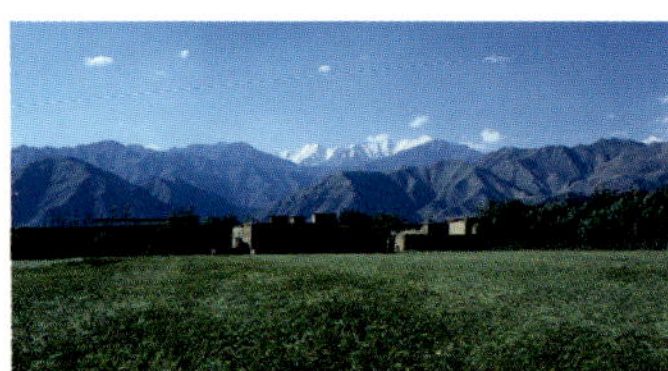

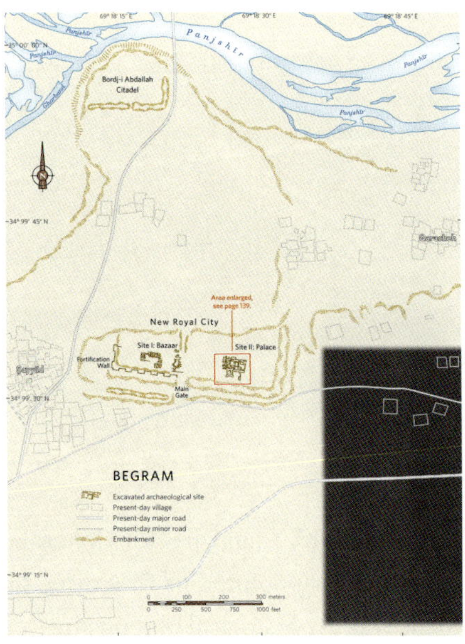

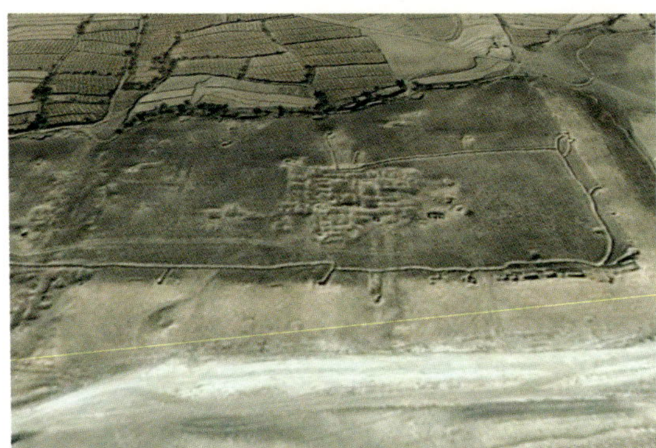

1940. Several areas were investigated, both inside and outside a rectangular walled area about half a kilometre across known as the 'New Royal City'. Part of a large building, most likely a palace, was extensively excavated and termed Site II.

Spectacular finds were made in two walled up strongrooms at the heart of this complex. Room 10 was excavated in 1937 and produced large numbers of bronze, alabaster, glass and ivory objects. Most of the ivories were found concentrated in the northern part and along the eastern edge of the room. They consisted of three spectacular caryatids (standing female figures), several furniture legs and a large number of plaques originally attached to foot stools placed in a line along the wall. The concentrations of finds were initially assigned group numbers and then re-numbered as individual pieces of furniture, e.g. Ensemble 325 was later defined as Foot Stool V.

Room 13 was excavated two years later and yielded similar items; but it also contained several large panels of openwork inlays forming chair backs, a collection of plaster moulds and numerous crushed Chinese lacquer bowls. The furniture had been either stacked or arranged facing one another. The finds were divided between the National Museum of Afghanistan in Kabul and the Musée Guimet in Paris; sometimes items from the same object were split between the two institutions.

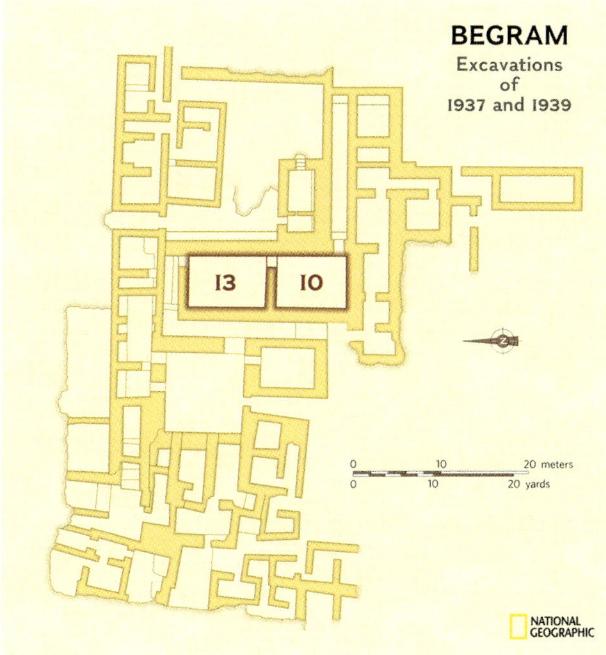

Plan of the excavated palace marking the two strongrooms.

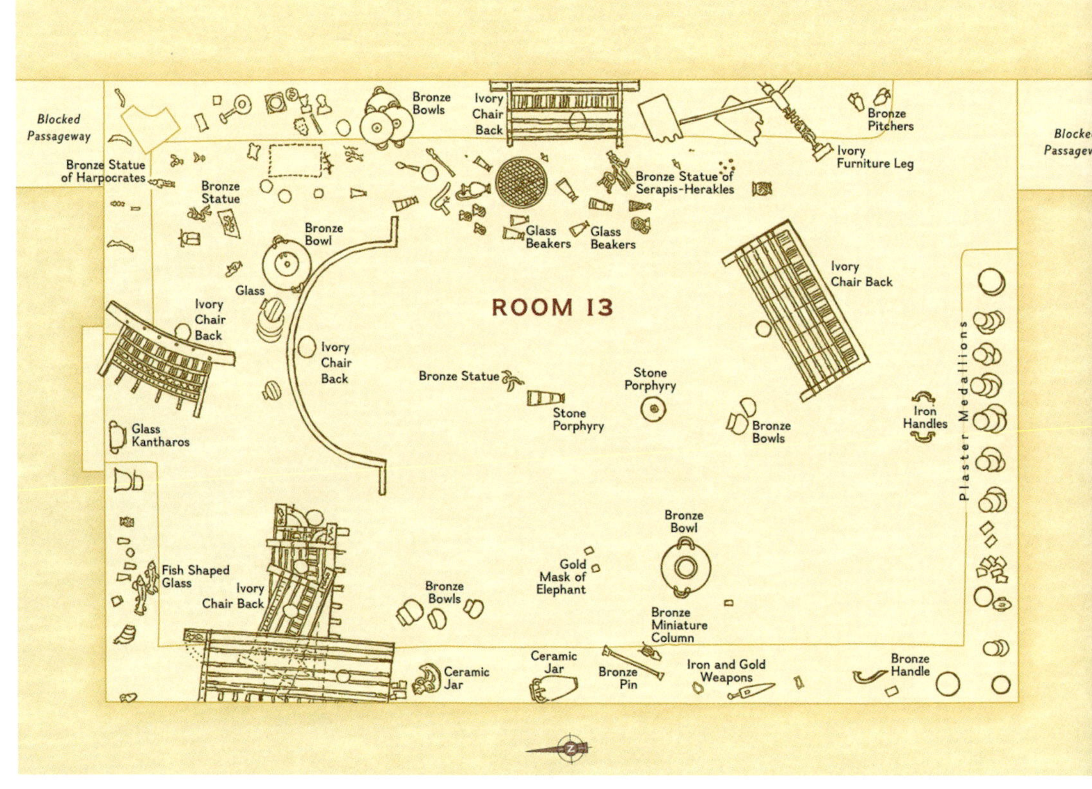

Following the outbreak of the Second World War the Hackins returned to France to join the 'Free French' resistance, but both died in 1941. Their deaths were a great loss for the final interpretation and publication of their excavations and their last season had to be prepared from their notes and was published posthumously in 1954. In the meantime, excavations were resumed at Begram in 1941 by Roman

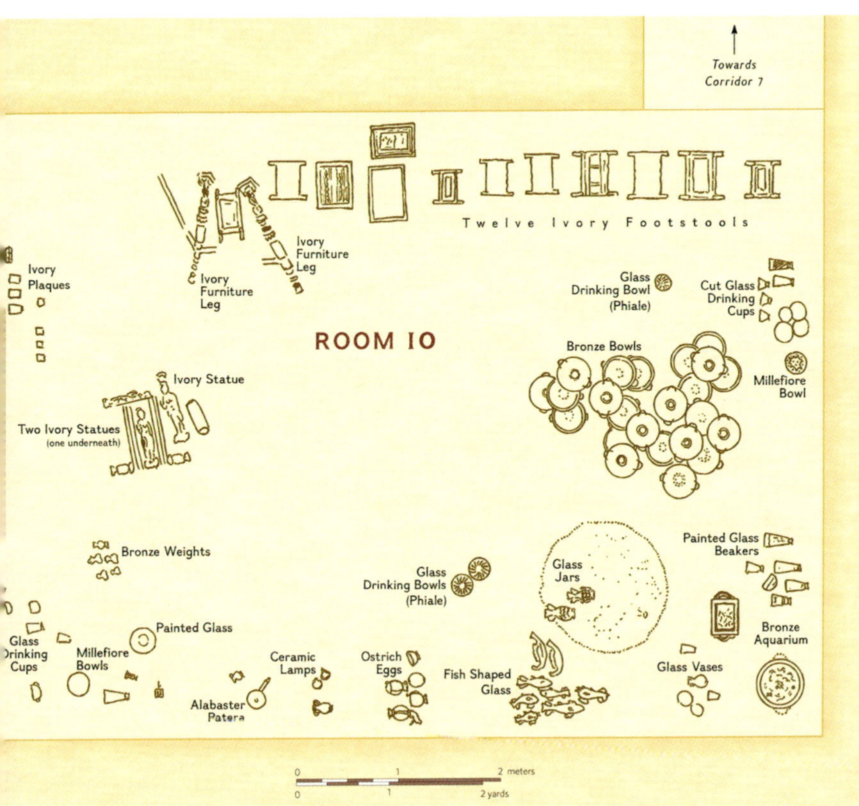

Plan of the excavated strongrooms marking the position of the Indian furniture and other items as they were found.

Ghirshman. He had previously excavated extensively in Iran and his main aim was to establish an archaeological sequence which would enable the finds from the previous excavations to be placed in a better historical context. He excavated both in the 'New Royal City' and the 'Old Royal City' at nearby Bordj-i Abdullah.

Ghirshman defined three periods of occupation at Begram

which he termed Niveaux I–III and dated through a combination of coin finds and historical assumption. The first period dates from the second century BC to the mid-second century AD. The site then appeared to be abandoned briefly before it was re-founded by the Kushan ruler Kanishka (*c.* 127–50). The previously excavated strongrooms were placed in this period with the idea that they had been hidden by the time of a hypothetical Sasanian sack in *c.* AD 241. Ghirshman's third stage was attributed to the Kushano-Sasanian period when Afghanistan was ruled by governors acting under the Sasanian empire of Iran, and was dated from the mid-third to late fourth centuries AD. During this period a small fort with circular corner towers was built over the remains of the earlier Kushan palace and helped to seal the strongrooms.

However, since Ghirshman, the final dating of the second period at Begram has been revised in the light of further research on the objects found in the two strongrooms. The Roman glassware, metalwork and carved stone vessels and Chinese lacquer found in these rooms have been re-dated to the first or possibly early second century. Previously published coin evidence of a third century date now appears to be unreliable as these coins actually come from later layers lying above the collapsed strongrooms. There is therefore no reason to tie the end of the palace (and Niveau II) to a mid-third century Sasanian sacking which was only hypothetical. We need another reason for the palace's abandonment.

The last excavations at Begram were carried out in autumn 1946. The 'New Royal City' was re-used subsequently for a military encampment, and trenches and foxholes are still clearly visible dug along the crest of the ancient fortifications. Despite (or because of)

this, the site has mercifully escaped the heavy looting which has
destroyed many hundreds of sites and monuments in Afghanistan
and it remains an outstanding candidate for renewed archaeological
excavation when future conditions permit.

2

The significance of the 'Begram ivories'

OVER a thousand ivory and bone inlays originally attached to wooden furniture were found in the two palace strongrooms at Begram. They are among the most important antiquities yet discovered in Afghanistan and are equally important for appreciating early Indian art of the first or possibly early second century.

The range of motifs includes female (rarely male) figures, mythical beasts, wildlife and floral designs. The female figures are the most popular subjects and are shown either singly or with attendants. They are depicted in loving detail with different hairstyles and items of personal adornment. Multiple bangles and prominent anklets are frequently shown and were presumably worn for their jingling effect, particularly as some of the figures are frozen in dance. Others are shown playing a variety of musical instruments, talking, or adjusting their hair or personal ornaments. A few carry weapons. The partial state of undress, distinctive earrings, decorated hairbows, beaded necklaces and hip girdles accentuating their bodies enhance a feeling of sensual luxury. Many figures are shown seated on woven wickerwork or more substantial furniture with lathe-turned legs framed within an architectural setting, sometimes with the doors ajar. Others are shown standing within an open gate corresponding to a distinctive Indian monumental type (*torana*) with three superimposed decorated architraves supported by carved uprights: this form is known in stone possibly as early as the Mauryan period but was probably more commonly carved from wood (which does not survive). Interpretations of these scenes vary: some see them as voyeuristic illustrations of life in a harem whereas others emphasize similarities with figures on Buddhist monuments.

The inlays are carved in different styles, which are sometimes combined on a single piece of furniture. A small number had incised or inked marks, including letters in Kharosthi, Brahmi (both originating in India) and a third, as yet unidentified, script. These were presumably fitters' marks designed to aid the assembly of complex pieces of furniture, but more study is required in order to understand them. The quality of workmanship is high and wherever they were made implies a confident artistic tradition which combines two-dimensional drawing and three-dimensional carving. They also imply a highly developed furniture-making tradition. Sir Max Mallowan's description in 1966 of a Jaipur ivory carving workshop he had visited creates an evocative picture of the sort of workshop which might have been involved, although not all details may have applied in antiquity:

I was told that the tusk was only considered mature at 50 years – that is the half-life of the male elephant. The craftsmen, incidentally, were all of humble origin; they were poorly paid

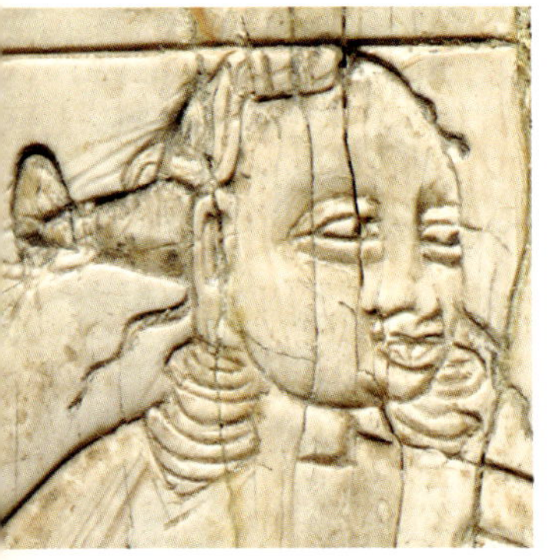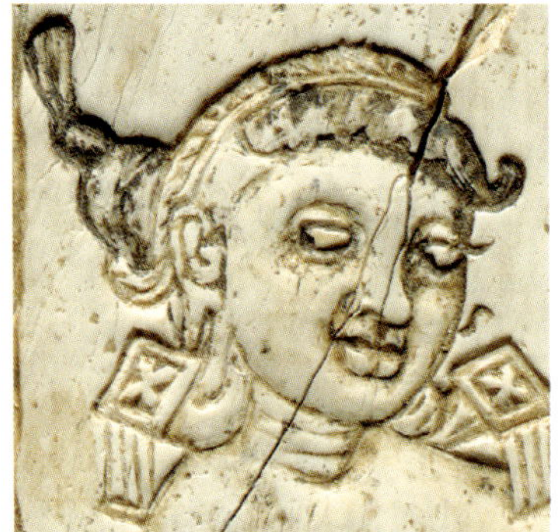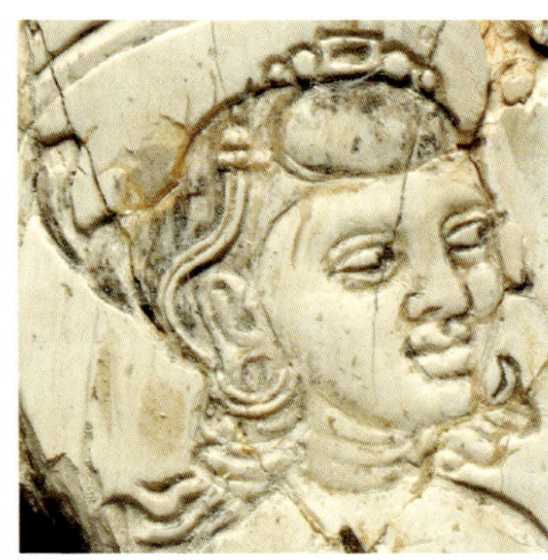

Details showing some of the faces of the women on the Begram ivories.

and their workshop was equipped only with a bare minimum of furniture; a single patron employed about twenty of them; some carvings could be achieved in a day, others required months of work according to their elaboration … the craftsman was only using chisel, file, fine saw and a nail with a sharp point, and a small tool with a flat paddle-shaped blade at each end … His practice was to saw a section longitudinally, cutting the tusk in two halves and then to make two similar figures after having sketched the object intended on the convex side … At Jaipur the craftsman said that the most delicate and tricky part of the operation was cutting out the open or *ajouré* parts of the figures … Such carvings were always more expensive owing to the risk of fracture. But if an accident happened, then the free-standing parts were altogether cut away, and only the solid figure was produced (Mallowan 1966: vol. II, 483–4).

In the case of the Begram inlays, both ivory and bone were carved in flat relief panels, often with two or three rectangular strips making up

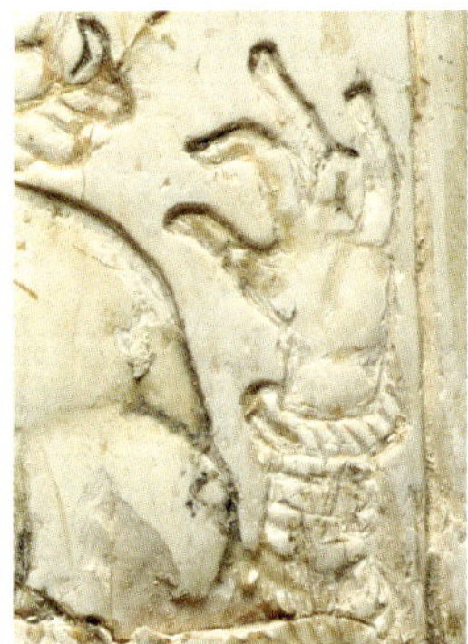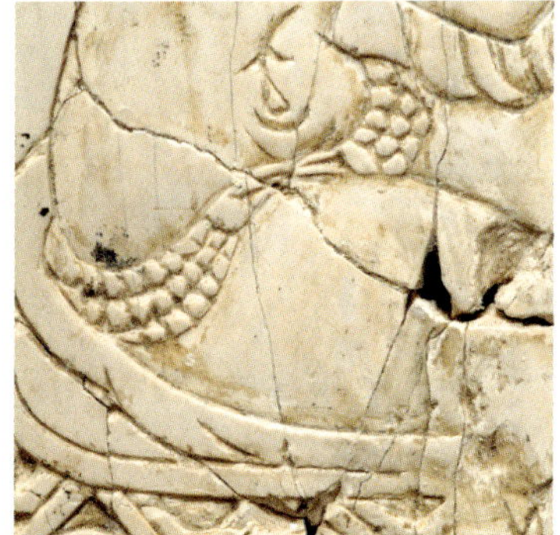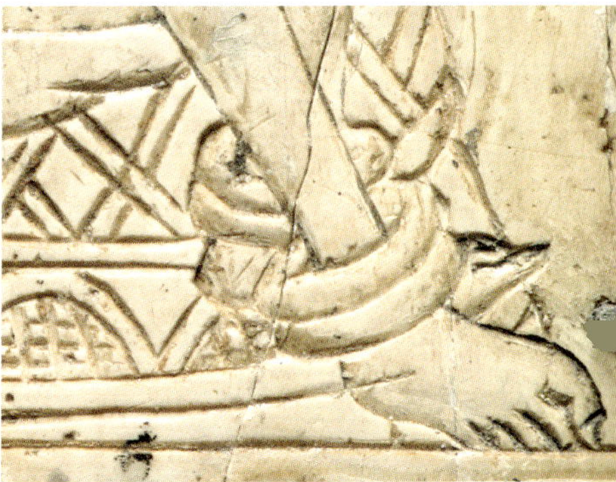

a single inlay; but only ivory, not bone, was suitable for openwork carving. Other ivory panels have a slightly convex profile which reflects the natural curvature of the tusk. The surfaces were smoothed and lightly polished after carving. Extensive traces of red pigment are visible on the slightly recessed backgrounds of many of the pieces carved in flat relief; red and blue were used to colour alternate quatrefoils decorating the borders of openwork carvings. On other plaques where the background was apparently left plain either red or black pigment was used, sometimes in combination, to highlight the incised outlines of the bodies, eyes and hair of human figures. This use of coloured pigments was normal in antiquity, whether on furniture or architecture.

The Begram inlays were originally attached to wooden furniture with tiny round-headed copper alloy rivets of varying size passed through pre-drilled holes: the use of bright yellow shiny metal (now corroded to green) would have added another dimension to their appearance. In addition, openwork was backed onto shiny sheets of mica which would have added a dramatic reflective background for,

Details showing items of personal adornment worn by the women on the ivories.

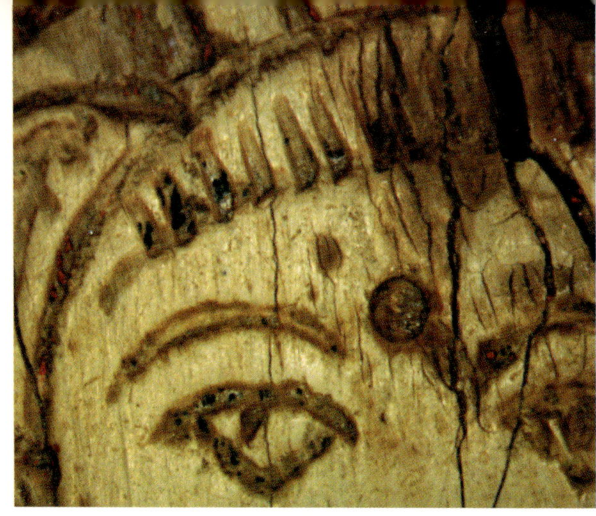

Macroscopic image of the hair of the central figure in 13. The dark blue material in the incised lines is indigo.

and depth to, the relief carving. Metal nails and long clamps were used to secure the different wooden elements. Unfortunately, by the time of excavation the woodwork itself had totally disintegrated and the colour, species and source used are therefore unknown. This has posed challenges in reconstructing the original appearance of many items. Some belonged to large chairs with high decorated backs, but many of the pieces found in Room 10 initially thought to be chests (*coffrets*) have since been re-interpreted as foot stools (*tabourets*) as they appear to be too narrow to be functional and there are no hinges or closing devices.

The origin of the pieces of decorative furniture has caused considerable disagreement since their discovery. They are stylistically Indian but there has been much controversy over their exact place of manufacture as well as their date. One reason is that there are relatively few early pieces of decorative carved ivory or bone surviving from India itself. The exceptions include two isolated ivory female statuettes (perhaps caryatids) found at Bhokardan and Ter, an ivory plaque from Kondapur, a spacer bead found at Śiśupālgarh which is

decorated with ducks and quatrefoils, and several other pieces
excavated at Taxila. The usual explanation given is that the climate
is too hot and humid for survival of archaeological ivory but other
factors should also be considered. Carved ivories are fragile and
normally only found archaeologically in sealed storerooms, wells
or destruction horizons at high-status sites where there has been
extensive excavation, and there have been few excavations of this
type in India. The main points of reference are therefore carved stone
monuments, particularly the Kushan centre of Mathurā (modern
Muttra) on the Jumna river and the Great Stupa at Sānchī in Bhopal,
both in north-central India. The latter was significantly enlarged in
the first century, and its massive carved stone gateways (*toranas*)
resemble both in outline and some details the miniature versions on
some of the Begram inlays. Moreover, the dedicatory inscription refers
tantalizingly to ivory carvers being involved in the construction: 'this
figure carving has been done by the ivory carvers of Vidiśā'. Other
parallels have been sought with later sculptures of the Satavahana
school at Amarāvatī and other centres in southern India. However,

Detail of one of
the ivories showing
the traces of the
original red pigment.

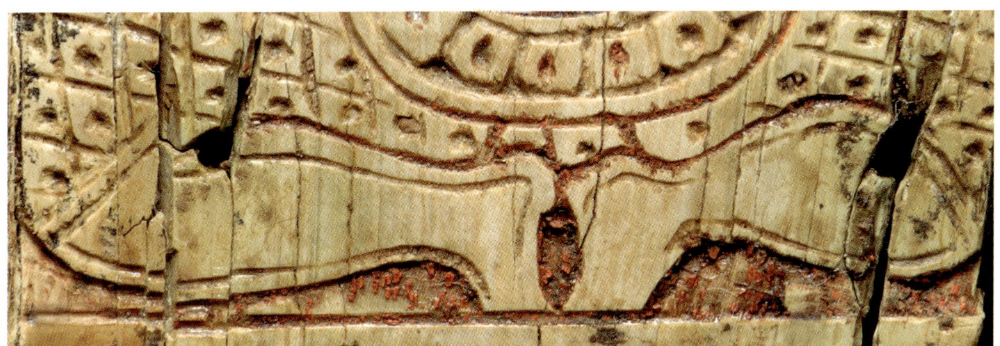

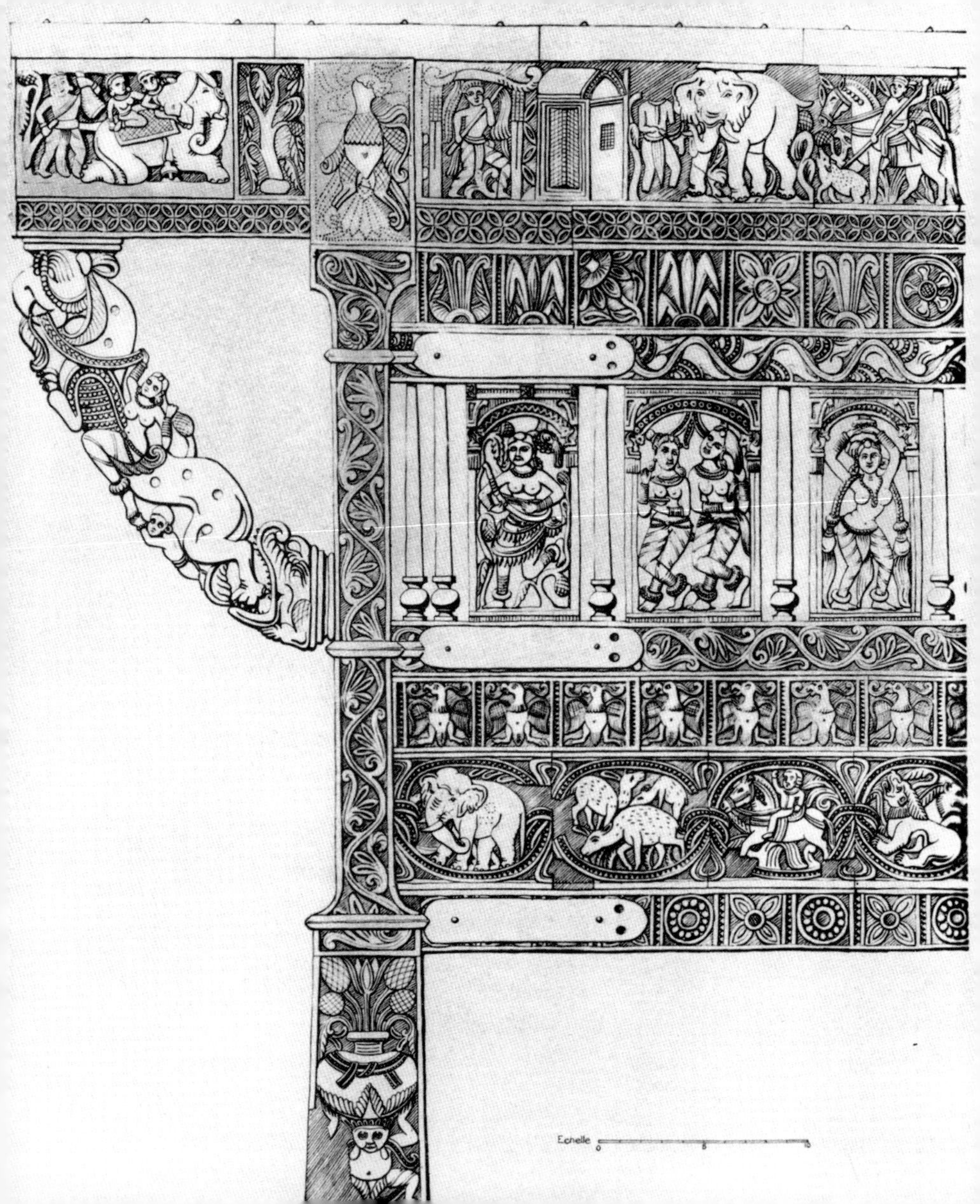
Echelle

all of these are religious monuments and the iconography is formulaic, whereas the Begram carvings seem to be for a secular context and details of the material culture represented are less likely to be archaizing. The problem is compounded by the use of several different styles of carving.

In his first report, the excavator Joseph Hackin proposed that the objects from Room 10 (the first of the strongrooms to be excavated) covered a wide date range between the first and fourth centuries, drawing parallels between some of the ivories (especially Foot Stool IX) and Gupta period art from Ajantā and Sānchī dating to about the same period. A late dating for Foot Stool IX was supported in 1974 by Elizabeth Rosen Stone who looked to parallels with Buddhist sculptures at Nāgārjunakonda in Andhra Pradesh (southern India), produced between c. AD 225 and 325. She has since found further parallels with sculptures on the stupa at Kanganhalli in Karnataka, dated between the first and early third centuries, including the depiction of similar hip girdles and vine scroll borders inhabited by small figures.

However, following excavations of the second strongroom in 1939, Hackin revised his opinion to propose that the finds belonged to the rise of the Kushan empire in the first or second century. After a detailed comparative analysis of motifs, personal ornaments and forms of hairstyle, in 1954 Philippe Stern placed most of the finds in the same period and intermediate between the 'old style' of Sānchī and the beginning of Mathurā style, but kept the later date for Foot Stool IX on the grounds that the creeping vine or acanthus scroll motif was not known any earlier. However, soon afterwards Otto Kurz observed that there were examples at Pompeii and so the motif was known in the Roman empire by the eruption of Mount Vesuvius in AD 79. A more extreme standpoint was taken by LeRoy Davidson who argued that the origins of this motif were Indian rather than Roman and that Foot Stool IX might be the earliest, rather than the latest, piece in the group.

A catalogue of contents known to have been in the National Museum in Kabul prior to 1985 was published in 2006 by Francine Tissot. She returned to a first to second century date for the Begram inlays and not only provided new reconstructions of the furniture but also drew more detailed parallels with luxury furniture (including thrones and foot stools) depicted on carvings from Mathurā and Amarāvatī. Recent research by Sanjyot Mehendale offers a detailed classification of subject matter and techniques but proposes a north-west Indian origin, perhaps including manufacture at Begram itself by craftsmen trained in or influenced by Indian styles. Mehendale also preferred a narrower first century date for all of the pieces on the assumption that the objects are contemporary with each other regardless of provenance. This research nevertheless provoked a lively riposte by Lolita Nehru who returned to Hackin's initial opinion of an early first to early third century date range and cited evidence from excavations at Sonkh in Mathurā to argue for a northern Indian origin for some pieces, while proposing a local Bactrian origin for others.

Not all of these differences of opinion can be resolved here but one point is clear. Extending the date of any of the ivories beyond the early second century is contradicted by the stratigraphic context of the coins and creates the problem of why there is nothing else of a comparably late date in these sealed strongrooms. It is reasonable to conclude therefore that the furniture is of one period and the variety of styles – often combined on a single piece of furniture – more probably reflects the dynamic cultural environment and high level of patronage afforded by the early Kushan rulers of the late first and/or early second century.

Indian epics contain frequent references to ivory in association with beds, couches, chairs, litters and portable objects; an inscription on the walls of a temple in Orissa records the gift of ivory [inlaid] couches; and the *Periplus of the Erythraean Sea*, a first century Romano-Egyptian account of Red Sea and Indian Ocean trade, refers to the north-west Indian coastal port of Barygaza as exporting ivory and the region of Dosarene (Orissa) as a source of beautiful ivory. The export of Indian furniture decorated with carved ivory in a similar style is archaeologically confirmed by a caryatid figure with a Kharosthi fitter's mark which was found in the Via dell'Abbondanza in Pompeii. Indian epics and Buddhist literature refer to the organization of ivory carvers (*dantakāra*) into guilds, an ivory carvers' bazaar at Benares and some ivory carvers also working in other materials, including conch shell and stone. The latter also helps explain the close similarity in style across media.

The range of objects found with the ivories at Begram suggests a strong cosmopolitan flavour and keen appreciation of luxuries by the local dynasts. This is vindicated by the *Periplus* which states in the case of Barygaza that 'For the king there was imported in those times precious silverware, slave musicians, beautiful girls for concubinage, fine wine, expensive clothing with no adornment, and choice unguent' (*Periplus* 49, transl. Casson 1989: 81).

3

Ivory and bone as sources of inlay

THE BEGRAM inlays were initially described as ivory but some were actually bone, and this applies also to some of the pieces discussed here. The distinction is not always easy to make and the wider archaeological literature contains many inaccuracies of identification. However, the choice of material was deliberate: they are of different value with different working properties, and their varying relative size enabled different styles and visual effects to be created.

Ivory was employed on the high visibility sections of the larger pieces of furniture at Begram. Ivory has been a desirable material for many thousands of years. As well as elephant, ivory has been (and continues to be) sourced from mammoth, walrus, narwhal and hippopotamus but elephant ivory is still considered to be the highest quality. India was of course a major supplier of elephant ivory but relatively little early ivory survives from India itself. However there are a number of finds from Afghanistan, Pakistan and Central Asia. The earliest are a partly worked tusk from Mehrgarh dating to the sixth millennium BC and a seal and gaming-piece from the site of Mundigak, near Kandahar, which date to *c*. 3000 BC. According to the foundation inscription of Darius I (*c*. 521–486 BC) from Susa, the eastern Achaemenid province of Arachosia (centred on Kandahar) was a source of ivory for the Achaemenid court, and a variety of ivory objects including hair combs and inlays were found in an Achaemenid palace well at Susa. Slightly later finds from the third century BC and first century AD include a short sword scabbard from Takht-i Sangin, one-piece hair combs decorated with engraved scenes, furniture legs from Ai Khanum which were turned on a lathe, and a series of magnificent drinking horns from Nysa. The source of the raw material must have been India but opinions differ as to whether some of the later finds – notably the hair combs – were imported ready made. One unique piece from the palace treasury at Ai Khanum which depicts a scene from an Indian epic is probably war booty seized in India by the Greco-Bactrian ruler Eucratides I (170–145 BC).

In the Near East and Egypt there was a very long tradition of employing ivory as a source of furniture inlay. Indian, African and the now extinct Syrian elephant were the main sources but hippopotamus ivory was also used. The largest number of finds comes from palaces and storerooms of the ninth-century BC Late Assyrian capital at Nimrud in present-day Iraq. These were carved in several different styles indicating different workshops in Assyria, northern and southern Syria and Phoenicia (present-day Lebanon). They were typically polychrome and were painted and decorated with gold or silver sheet overlays and glass (less commonly semi-precious stone) inlays set in a coloured bedding material, and often have fitters' marks on the reverse. In the case of Nimrud, much of the furniture had fallen out

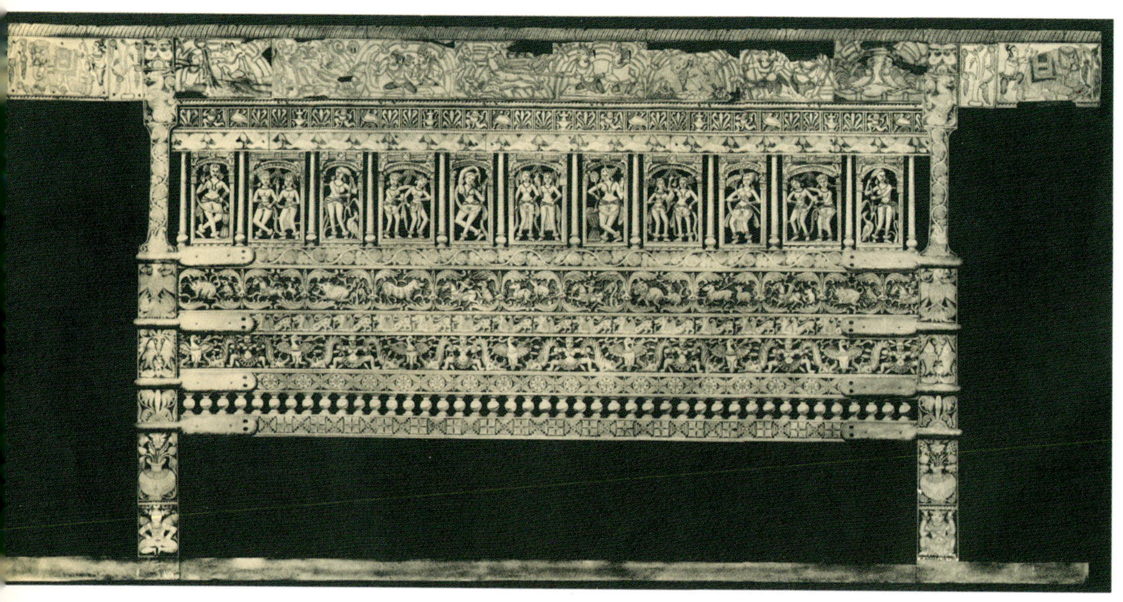

of fashion by the time of the sack of the city in 612 BC and the partly dismantled pieces were found in storerooms where they had been left after recycling their inlays.

At Begram, bone inlays were used either on the foot stools or on the lower visibility elements of the large chairs. This suggests that there was a hierarchy of materials. In contrast to ivory, bone was always easy to get hold of, and workshops probably obtained it immediately after butchers or leatherworkers had slaughtered the animals. Cooked bone is usually useless for carving as it is discoloured and chemically altered, so there would be little point in scavenging middens for re-use. Bone was first used in the Near East and South Asia for making small personal ornaments as it was easily worked but, following improvements in technology and exchange networks, it was generally dropped in favour of brighter materials such as coloured stones, or artificial materials such as glazed composition or glass. Nevertheless it continued to be suitable for making durable pointed items such as awls and hair pins, or for splitting into flat plates which could be used for inlaying. These lend themselves to engraved decoration.

4

Conservation and scientific research

THE CONSERVATION of archaeological ivory can be very complex and time-consuming. Organic materials such as bone and ivory are very fragile, with ivory particularly susceptible to splitting along the natural growth lines of the dentine which forms the tusk; unsurprisingly these inlays were found in a highly fragmented and extremely poor state of preservation. Different pieces of furniture had also been laid on top of one another and determining the overall appearance of these still poses problems. In order to stabilize the ivory fragments sufficiently to allow them to be cut out of the soil with a palette knife, Jean Carl, one of the excavators, devised a technique involving pouring layers of warm gelatine on to the ivories, followed by tissue. Once lifted, the secured fragments were then carefully turned over and the process repeated on the other side.

This process made them stronger for lifting but resulted in the formation of a hard surface layer which also trapped any dirt and possibly caused movement of loose pigment on the surface.

Unfortunately gelatine itself is an unstable material and will shrink and become brittle over time. The shrinking of the gelatine can result in the lifting and flaking of the fragile ivory surface. Over time further coatings have been applied, presumably in an attempt to rectify this problem and prevent further deterioration. These coatings have themselves degraded and give the surface an unnatural shine, obscure surface detail, and absorb dust and dirt. However, since all these treatments are primarily superficial, the interior of the object has remained very weak and fragile. Cracks and breaks have been joined in the past with a variety of adhesives and without prior consolidation of the fragile join edges. This has left the joins very susceptible to further failure. Repeated re-attachment has resulted in multiple layers of glue that have led to increasingly weak joins and more inaccurate reconstructions. Attempts were made to support the objects using a variety of materials including fabric, wax, 'superglue' and gesso backings. In addition, there was an accumulation of hair and cotton wool deposits as the remnants of previous surface treatments.

With the permission of the authorities at the National Museum in Kabul, these objects were examined in the Department of Conservation and Scientific Research at the British Museum. This was essential in order to prepare the pieces for display and travel. It also enabled work to understand the state of degradation of the ivories, the previous conservation treatments, the identification of materials, their technique of manufacture and the characterization of remaining traces of polychromy. The ivories were examined by optical microscopy and in ultraviolet light. Although most appear reasonably intact,

The condition of one of the Begram ivories (14) before recent conservation.

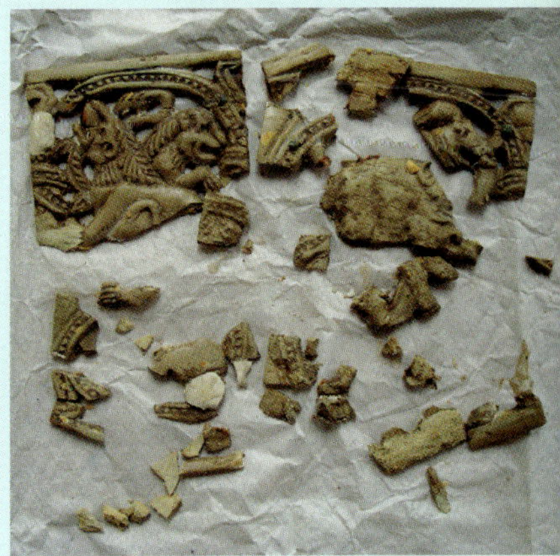

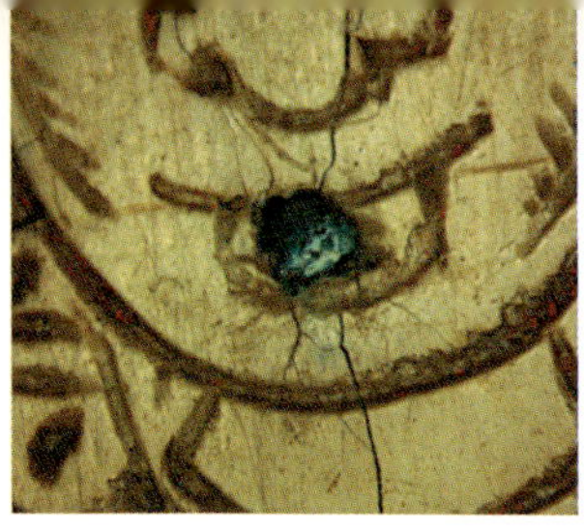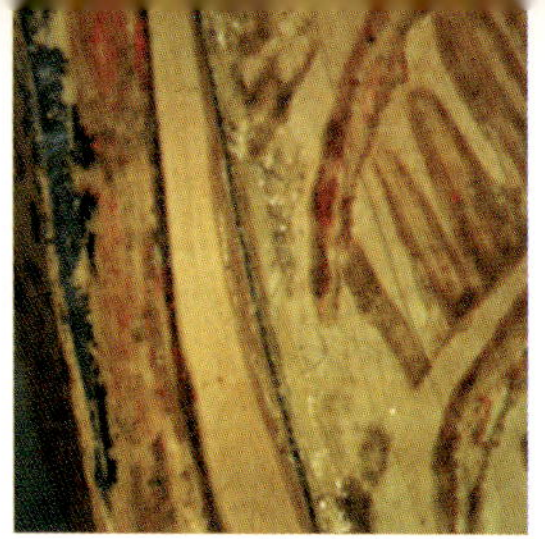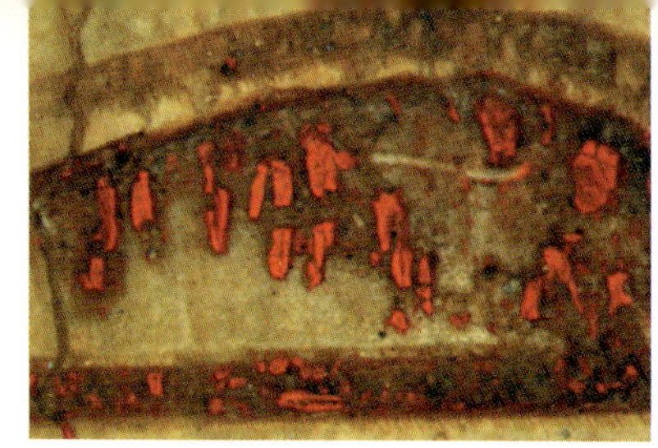

One of the Begram ivories has traces of the original vermilion and indigo pigment (below). The suggested digital recolouring (right) is based on these surviving remains. The details (above) show the central metal pin and macroscopic images of the top left hand corner and bottom.

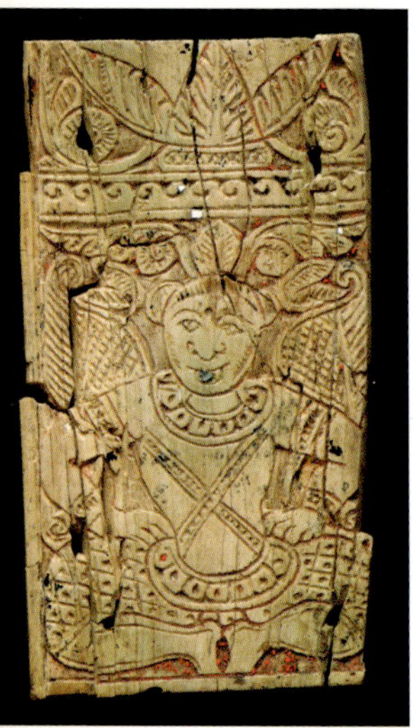

the delicate state of the inlays can be seen clearly in X-radiographs.

Shiny, unstable surface coatings and other extraneous surface deposits were removed where possible using appropriate solvents applied with cotton wool buds. All treatments were carried out under magnification. Fragile pieces were consolidated as necessary. Joins were investigated, strengthened and improved where possible. In some cases missing areas were filled where it was important to give support to the rest of the object. These fills were toned in with matching colours. All adhesives, resins and fills consisted of stable reversible resins compatible with the fragile ivory substrate.

Ivory is best stored and displayed in an environment where the relative humidity and temperature are stable: 40–55 per cent relative humidity and a temperature of 16–20°C are generally recommended. Lighting levels, and particularly the ultraviolet light levels, should also be limited, particularly for polychrome ivories.

At the time of writing, it has only been possible to look in detail at three of the pieces (**11**, **13**, **17**), but many intriguing details have already been revealed about how they were decorated. The liberal use of the gelatine consolidated the pieces sufficiently for them to be excavated and lifted, but its presence prevents any attempt to characterize the organic binding medium associated with the pigments. Nevertheless, for the first time the pigments associated with the extensive traces of colour visible with the naked eye on these three ivories have been conclusively identified.

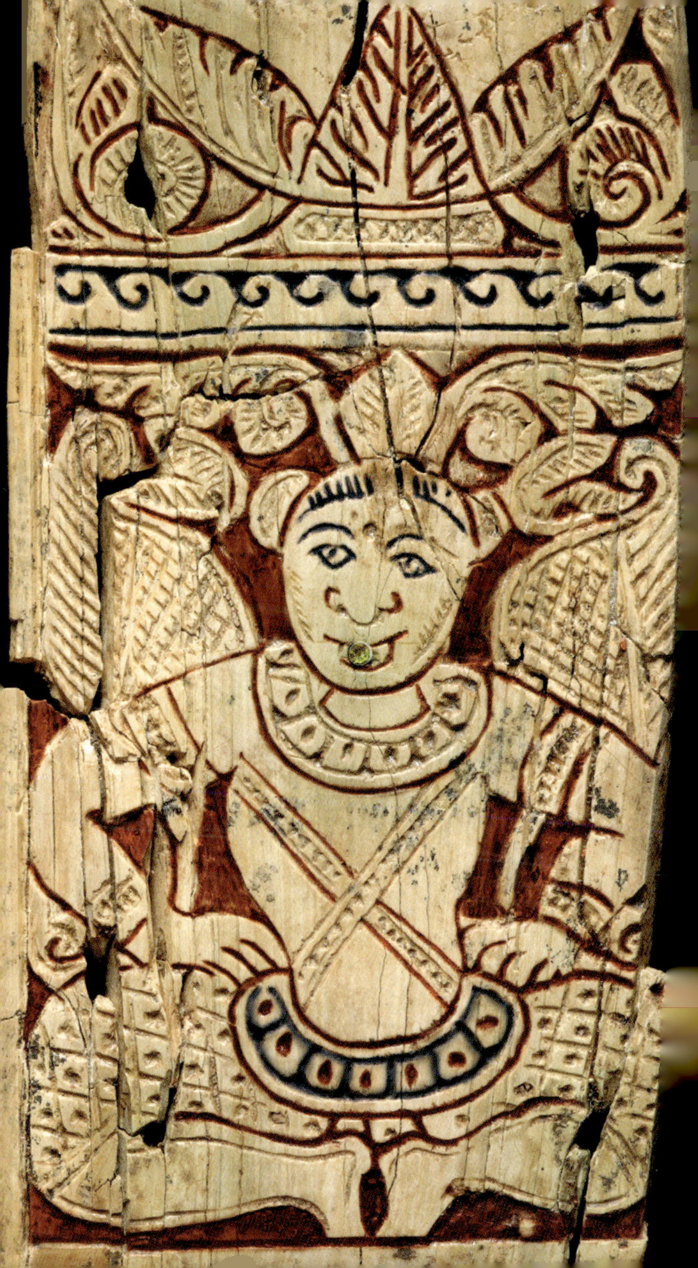

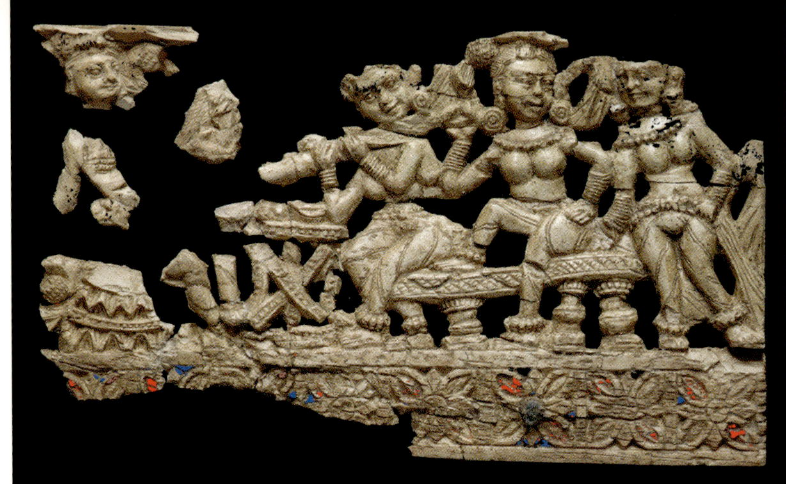

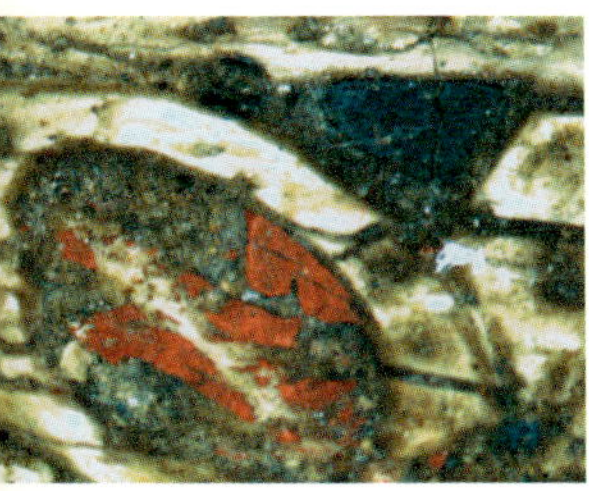

The floral border on this ivory (17) has remains of original pigment. The macroscopic image of a detail of this (above) shows vermilion (red) and indigo (blue) in the recessed shapes.

The colour traces have been mapped using a combination of microscopic examination and multi-spectral imaging techniques. The latter employ infrared and ultraviolet radiation, ranges of the electromagnetic spectrum that are not visible with the human eye, to reveal features that are often invisible to the naked eye. In this ay traces of four different coloured materials, red, dark blue and two types of black, have been located. The pigments used in each case have been identified using two non-contact, non-destructive analytical techniques, Raman spectroscopy and X-ray fluorescence analysis. The red found on the three inlays examined is vermilion. It appears most commonly to have been used to highlight the backgrounds, where it is thickly applied into deliberately recessed areas. The blue pigment associated with the quatrefoil decoration on the border of inlay **17** is indigo. Here, like the vermilion, it is thickly applied to a recessed area, but it also appears, applied more lightly, in incised lines. The black material found in other incised lines is carbon based, but at this early stage it is difficult to be sure if this was applied as a deliberate pigment, or if it represents dirt that has become trapped in the engraving over time. A second black material, rather smudgy in appearance, occurs on all three of the objects examined. This material has a fairly random distribution that does not respect the design: analysis showed it to be composed of manganese oxides, making it likely that it was deposited on the inlays by natural processes during burial.

The identification of the pigments vermilion and indigo does not assist directly with the origin or dating of the inlays, with both materials being available in India or locally. Vermilion (mercury sulphide) exists as the mineral cinnabar but was also produced artificially from antiquity. The presence of indigo, an organic pigment derived from plants of the *Indigofera* species, is more unexpected, given the ready availability of a range of mineral or inorganic blue pigments (including lapis and Egyptian blue). However, the first-century trade account known as the *Periplus* refers to the ports of Barbarikon (at the mouth of the Indus), Muziris and Nelkynda (on the Coromandel coast) as exporting 'Chinese pelts, cloth, and yarn; indigo', thus confirming the availability of indigo (*Periplus* 39, transl. Casson 1989: 75).

Given the presence of at least two deliberate colours it seems likely that other, possibly less stable, pigments might have originally been used, although no definitive evidence has yet been found. None the less it has been possible to use information gained from this investigation to digitally recolour one of the pieces and give at least a partial impression of its original appearance.

Many of the inlays still retain the metal pins used to hold them in place on the furniture. These now show heavy green corrosion, suggesting that they are made of copper or a copper alloy. Analysis of these materials is at a very early stage but already differences in composition have been noted.

5

Catalogue of the individual pieces

TWENTY inlays from the palace strongroom at Begram are presented here, some published for the first time. Eleven belong to foot stools excavated in Room 10 in 1937, including four which belong to Foot Stool I and either show individually carved scenes of seated women (**1–3**) or a bird standing on a lotus (**11**). Four others show individually carved designs of a *makara* (an Indian mythological beast) or animated ducks and were part of Foot Stool V (**7–10**). Another three inlays belonged to Foot Stool IX, one of the most famous items from Begram, and show flirtatious dancing women (**5–6**) and a playful lion (**12**).

Two openwork inlays showing female musicians and a woman beneath a gateway belong to either Chair 1 or 4 which were found in Room 13 in 1939 but, as these two pieces of furniture were stacked on top of each other, it is still not clear which pieces went with what (**17–18**). Two other inlays belonged to Chairs 2 and 3, which were found in the same room and are decorated with a squatting tree spirit (**13**)

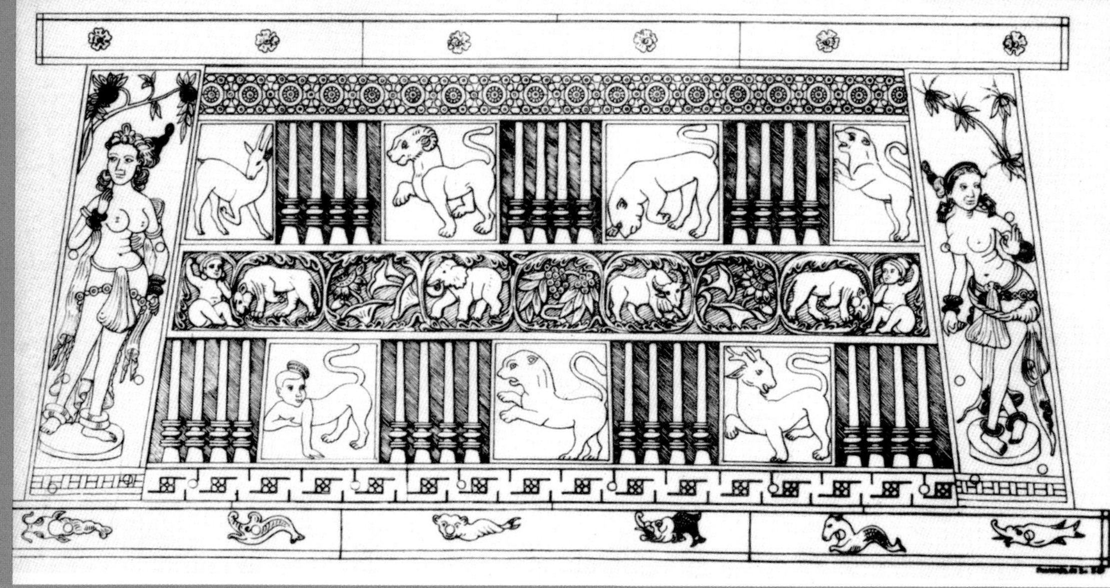

and a pair of roundels enclosing lions and an elephant (**14**). A plaque
and a fragmentary openwork frieze each depict scenes of riders, in the
first case with women on the back of an elephant (**15**), the other with
female figures riding mythical beasts (**16**). These resemble other
published pieces from Rooms 13 and 10 but exactly which pieces of
furniture they belonged to is uncertain. A single openwork plaque
showing a female gate guardian with a spear is similar in style to the
inlays used on Chairs 1 or 4 but was part of a larger plaque (**19**).

Finally, as two of the remaining inlays were not published in the
original excavation reports, they cannot be connected with specific
pieces of furniture: they include a lively scene of a woman toying with
a parrot (**4**) and a carved furniture element (**20**).

Reconstruction by
Pierre Hamelin of
Foot Stool IX.

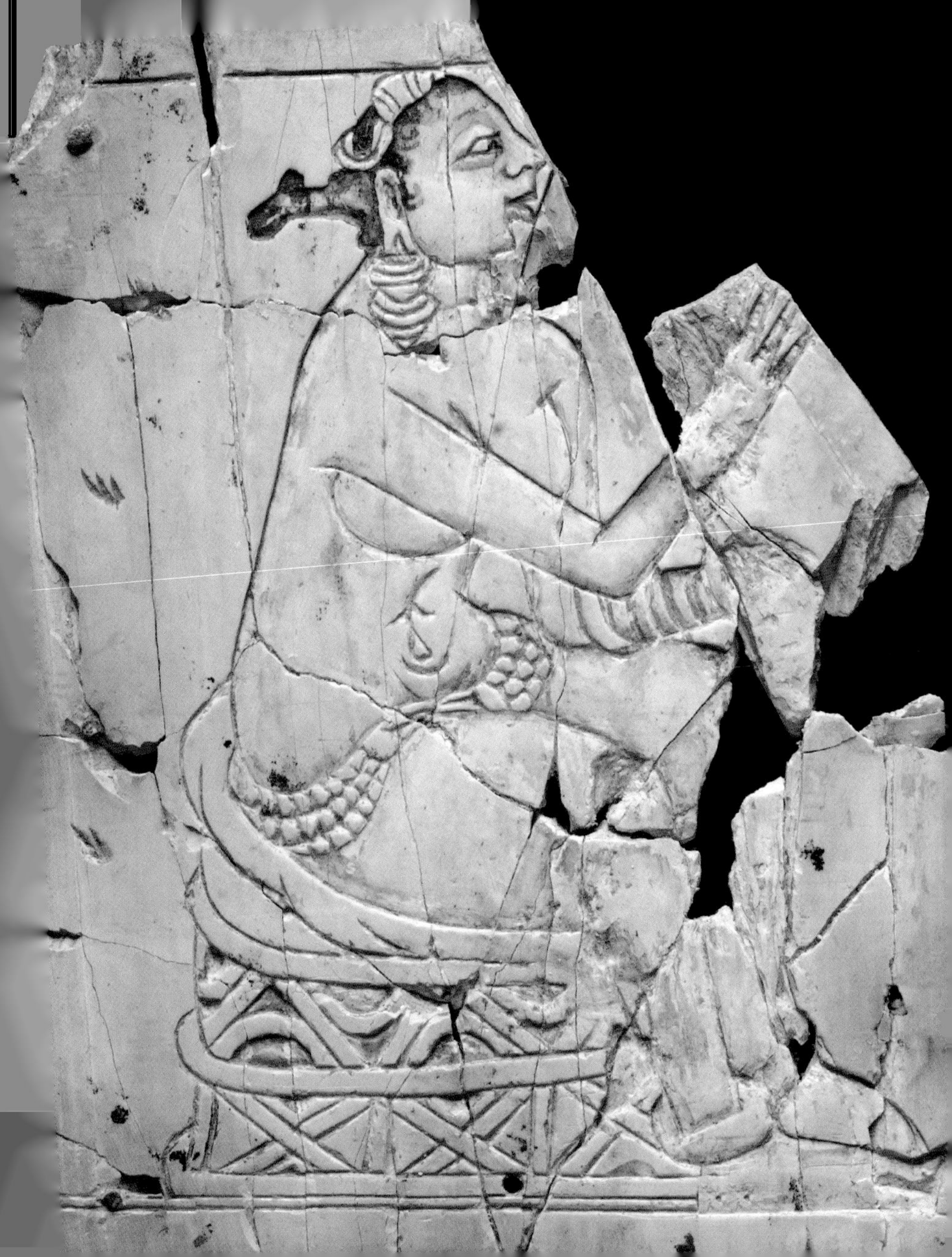

Seated woman, right profile

H 7.8 × W 6 × Th 0.3 cm
Room 10, Group 321, Foot Stool I
K.M. inv. no. 59–1–16
Hackin 1939: 68–9, pl. XL, fig. 85

A rectangular incised ivory inlay originally secured to an item of wooden furniture with tiny copper alloy tacks, measuring 0.1 cm across, passed through circular holes drilled around the edges. A single horizontal incised line frames the scene at top and bottom and encloses a woman with a tightly bound ponytail and heavy earrings seated cross-legged on a low stool, her modesty neatly concealed by her gesture and a three-row beaded hip girdle. Her animated hands emphasize what she is saying.

The stool appears to be woven wickerwork and precisely the type of light portable furniture which is a typical Indian craft tradition but vulnerable to termites and so does not survive in the archaeological record. Other types of thrones, stools, tables, decorated cushions and soft bolsters are depicted on Indian sculptures from Mathurā and Amarāvatī and later cave paintings at Ajantā, but none closely resemble the reconstructed pieces from Begram.

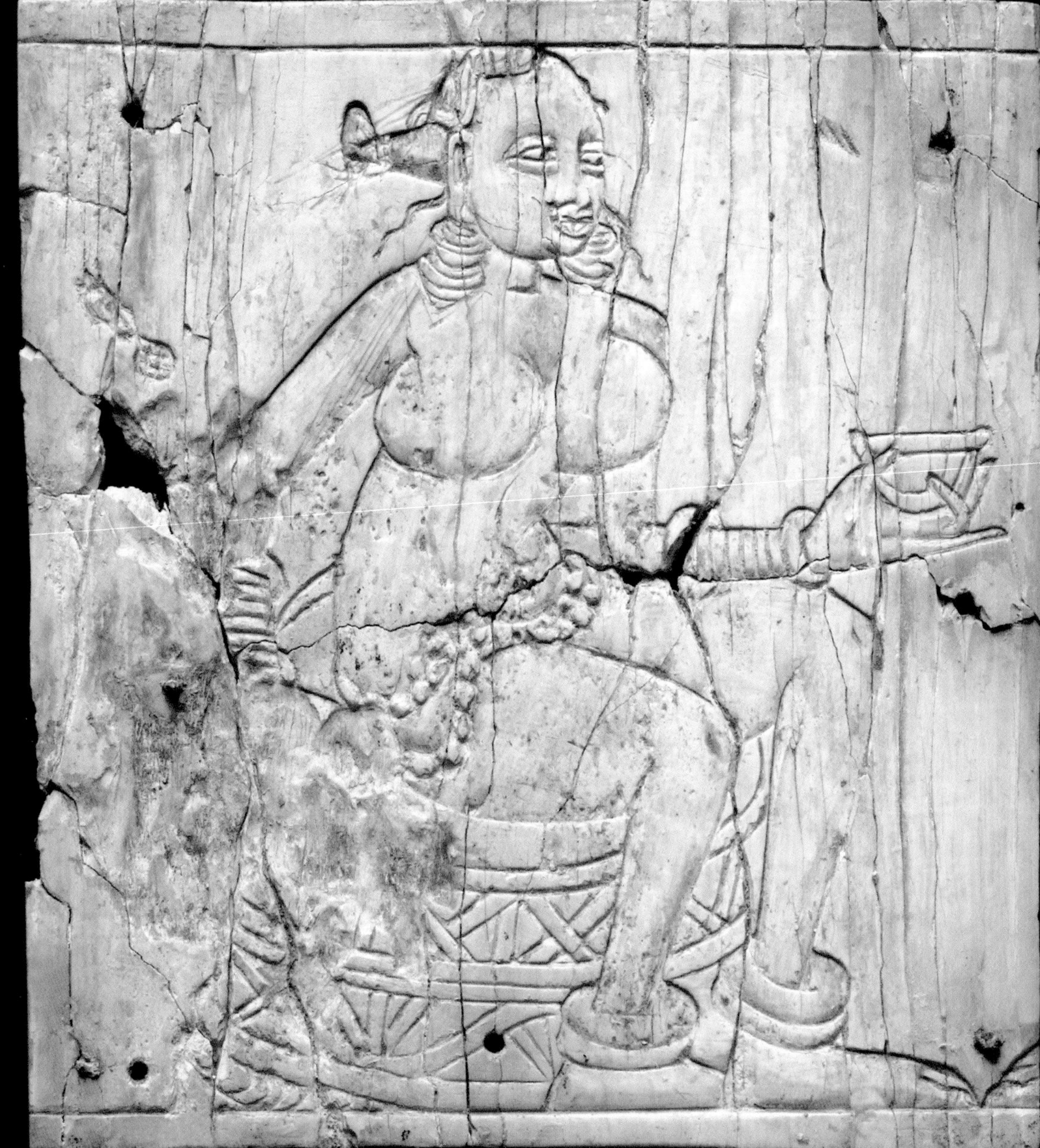

2 *Seated woman holding a bowl*

H 7.9 × W 7.2 × Th 0.2 cm
Room 10, Group 321, Foot Stool I
K.p.Beg.281.21; K.M. inv. no. 59–1–12
Hackin 1939: 68, pl. XL, fig. 84; Tissot 2006: 144; Rosen Stone 2008: fig. 15

Incised ivory inlay showing a nude seated woman holding a bowl, and framed top and bottom by a single horizontal incised line. This was originally part of Foot Stool I and attached by means of small copper alloy tacks measuring 0.1 cm across. The style of her hair, earrings and stool are identical to **1** but she is also wearing a pair of heavy anklets on each leg and a row of bangles on each lower arm. Traces of black pigment survive on the hair.

The anklets were probably hollow and made of metal. For example, a pair of silver anklets found at Taxila, in a hoard concealed in the mid-first century, are decorated in repoussé and have small loops for attaching bells or pendants which would have created a pleasant sound in motion. Many of the women depicted on the Begram ivories are also wearing multiple bangles on their forearms. These are usually of uniform size but occasionally with a larger example at each end. There was no attempt to add incised detail or, apparently, colour on these. Similar bangles are shown being worn by *yakshis* (tree spirits) on the Great Stupa at Sānchī and an ivory caryatid, 25 cm high (originally misidentified as a mirror handle) found at Pompeii.

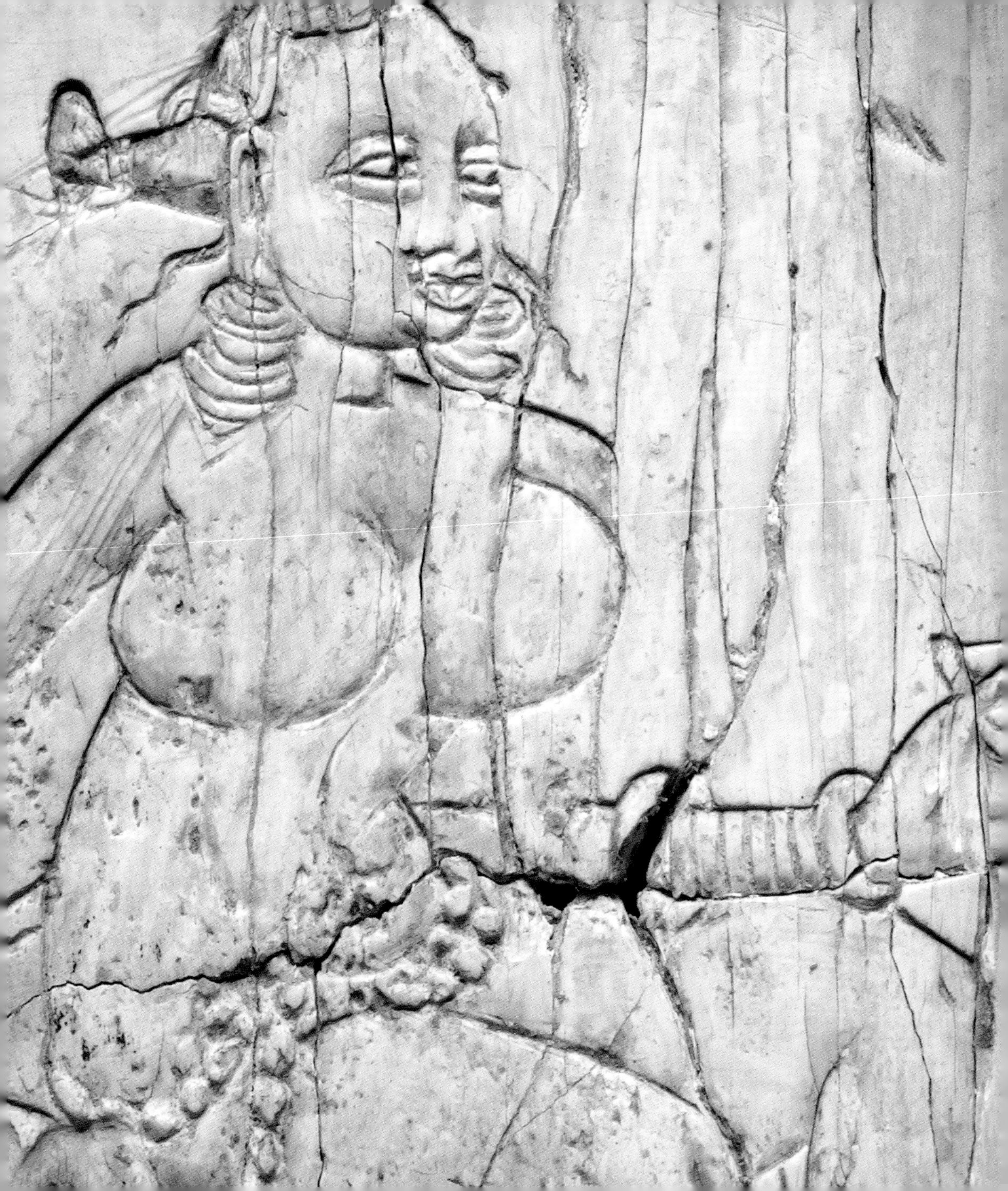

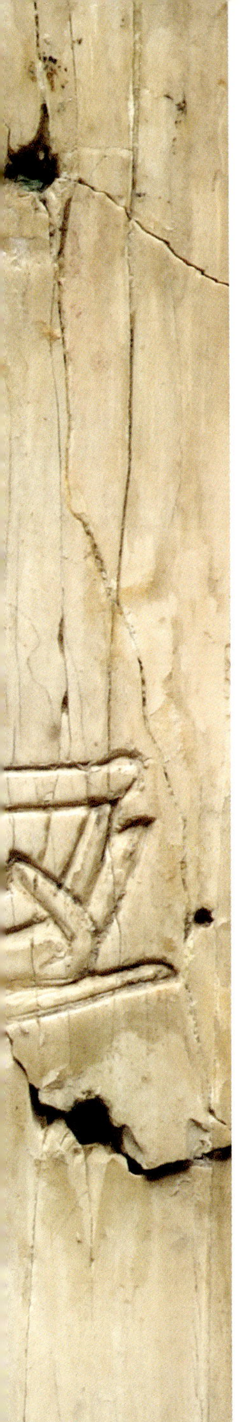

Glass bangles are very popular in India today but this industry does not pre-date the early medieval period. Before that conch-shell and ivory bangles were popular; this explains why some of the glass bangles imitate the shape of their forerunners. Evidence for ivory bangle carving has been found at Nevasa and dated to between *c.* 50 BC and AD 200, and some were painted red. The combination of anklets and bangles would have been particularly appropriate for dancers and attendants, and is consistent with their frequent depiction on the inlays from Begram.

3 *Seated woman, looking to her right*

H 7 × W 6.2 × Th 0.1 cm
Room 10, Foot Stool I
K.p.Beg.279.19; K.M. inv. no. 59–1–13
Tissot 2006: 143

Fragmentary incised ivory inlay showing a nude woman seated on a
woven wickerwork stool, with her body turned in mid-conversation.
It was originally square and part of Foot Stool I, and was secured with
six tiny copper alloy pins measuring 0.1 cm across which were
arranged in two rows running down each side.

The effective way in which the figure is carved creates a delightful
sense of movement and engages the viewer. The woman is depicted as
nude apart from a broad hip girdle, presumably intended to illustrate
a sash of woven cloth, held in the centre with a long narrow metal
clasp. Remains of dark pigment survive in the hair and incised outline
of the body.

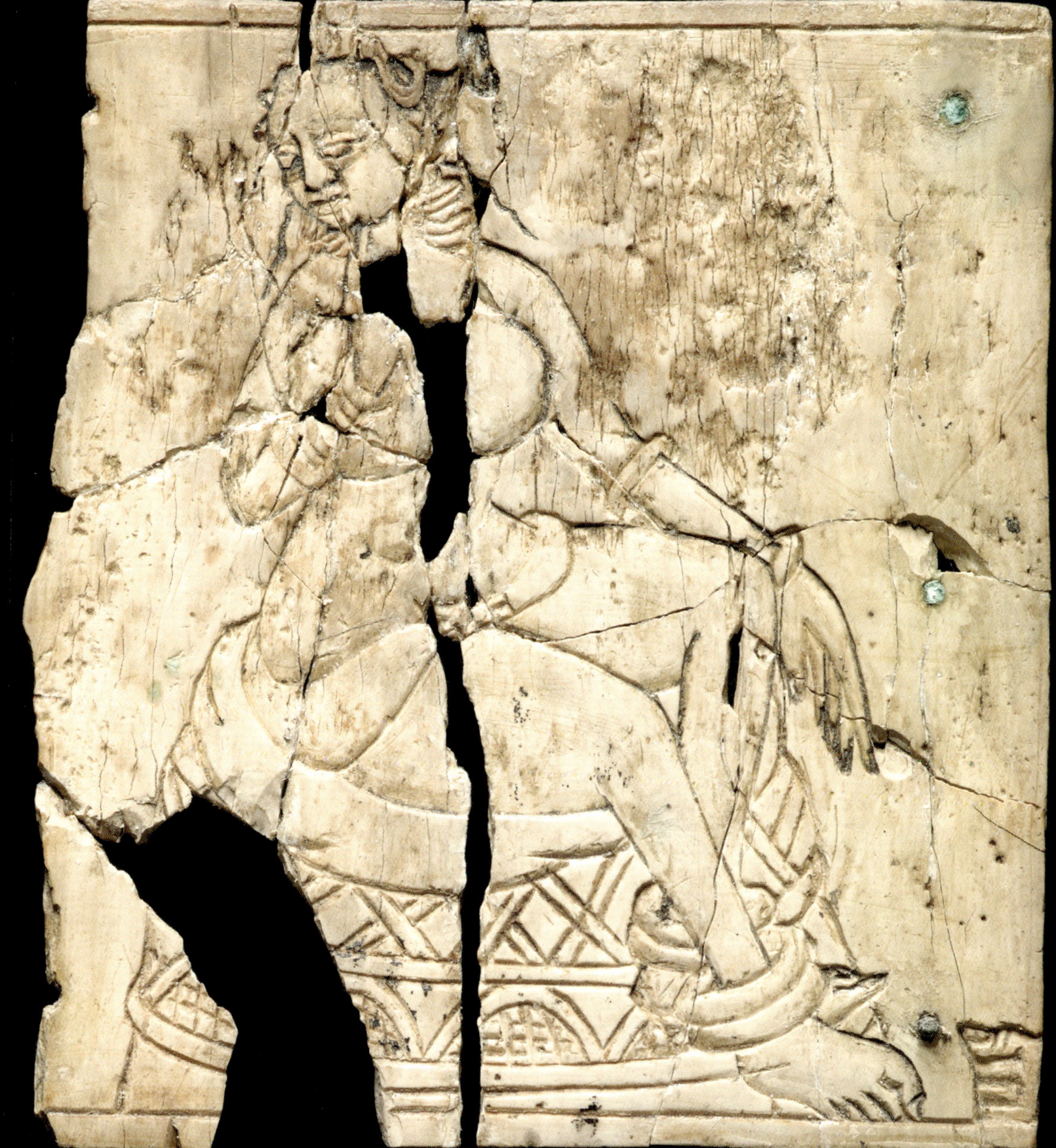

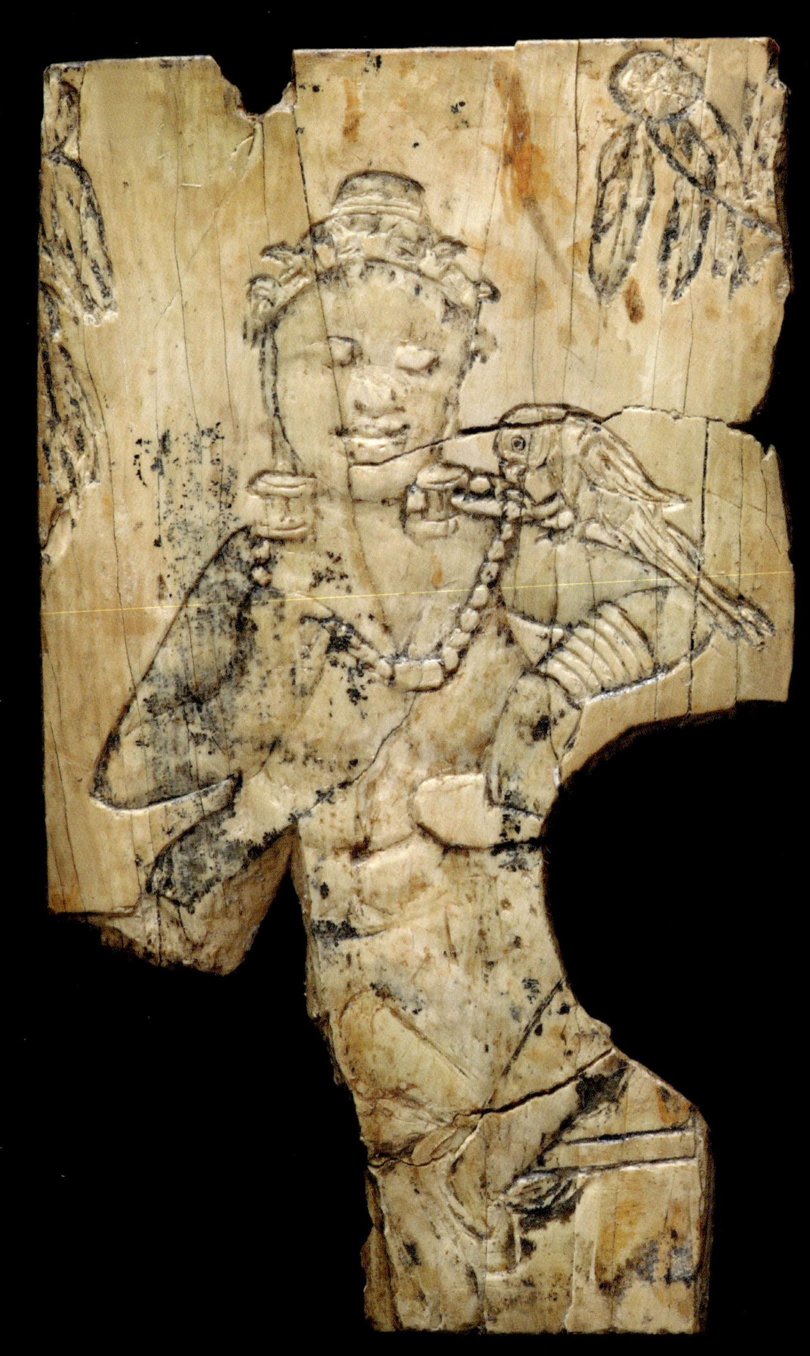

4 *Female figure toying with a parrot*

H 7.4 × W 4.4 × Th 0.3 cm
Previously unpublished

Incised ivory inlay showing a nude cross-legged woman wearing a necklace of large beads with a rectangular central setting that is being played with by a parrot seated on her left shoulder. She is wearing very distinctive heavy spool-shaped earrings with her hair piled up behind a bow, multiple bangles on each wrist and is holding what appears to be a small bottle in her left hand. There are traces of dark pigment in the incised outline of her body and on her hair.

The relatively large size and ovoid shape of the beads suggests these are intended to be semi-precious stones rather than pearls, coral, glass micro-beads or shell discs, all of which were also popular in India at this period. A range of semi-precious stones is mentioned in the *Periplus,* including turquoise and lapis lazuli exported from Barbarikon on the lower Indus and onyx and agate from Barygaza on the north-west Indian coast. The source of the turquoise was north-east Iran or Central Asia and it was a popular type of jewellery inlay judging by the contemporary first century graves at Tillya Tepe. The lapis, also used for inlay, originated from mines at Sar-e Sang in Badakhshan, and the export of both gemstones into India must therefore have been under Kushan control. By contrast, the listing of onyx and agate (popular local Indian bead materials) as specialities of Barygaza reflects the area's proximity to the major source of these varieties of chalcedony in the Deccan region of central India.

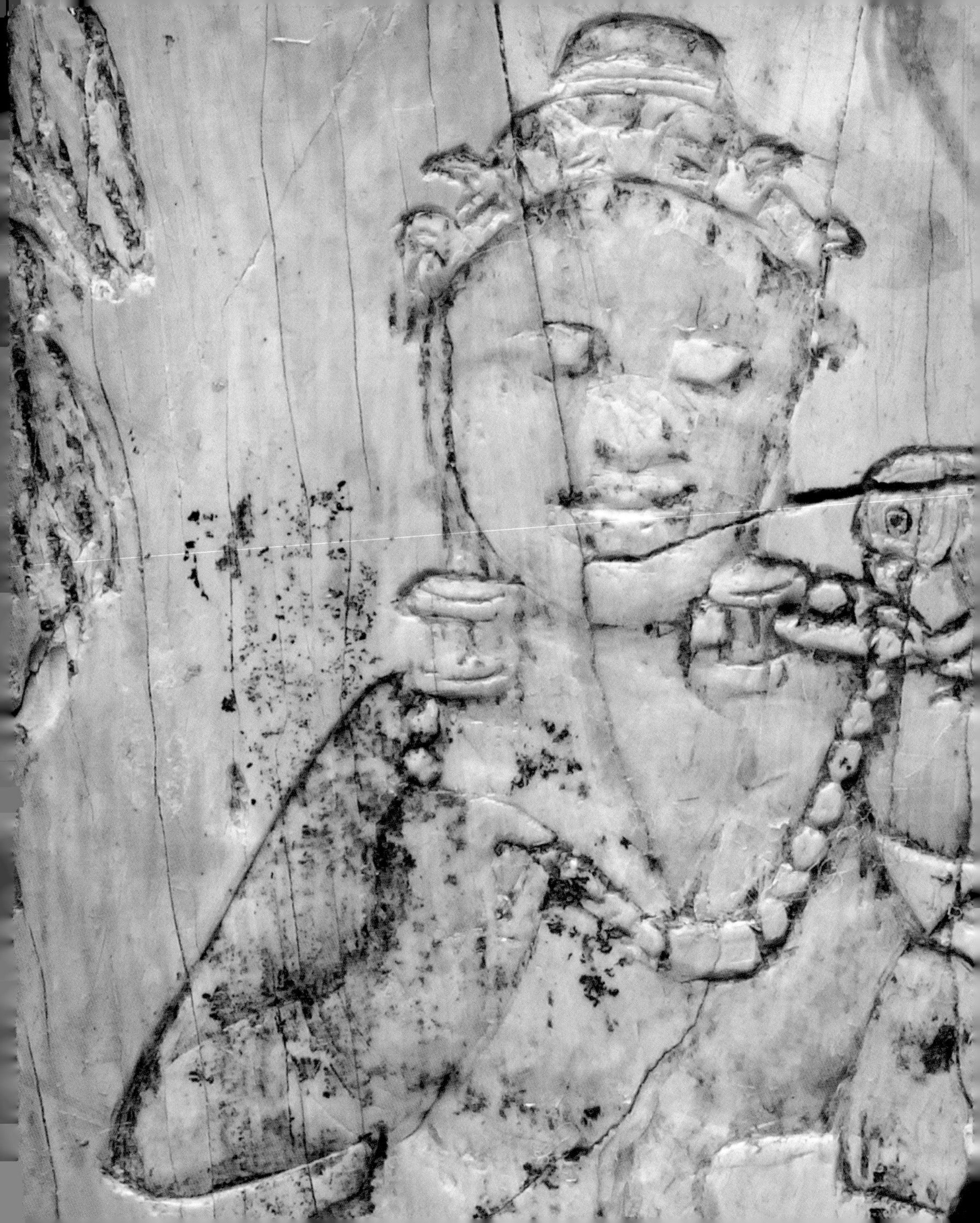

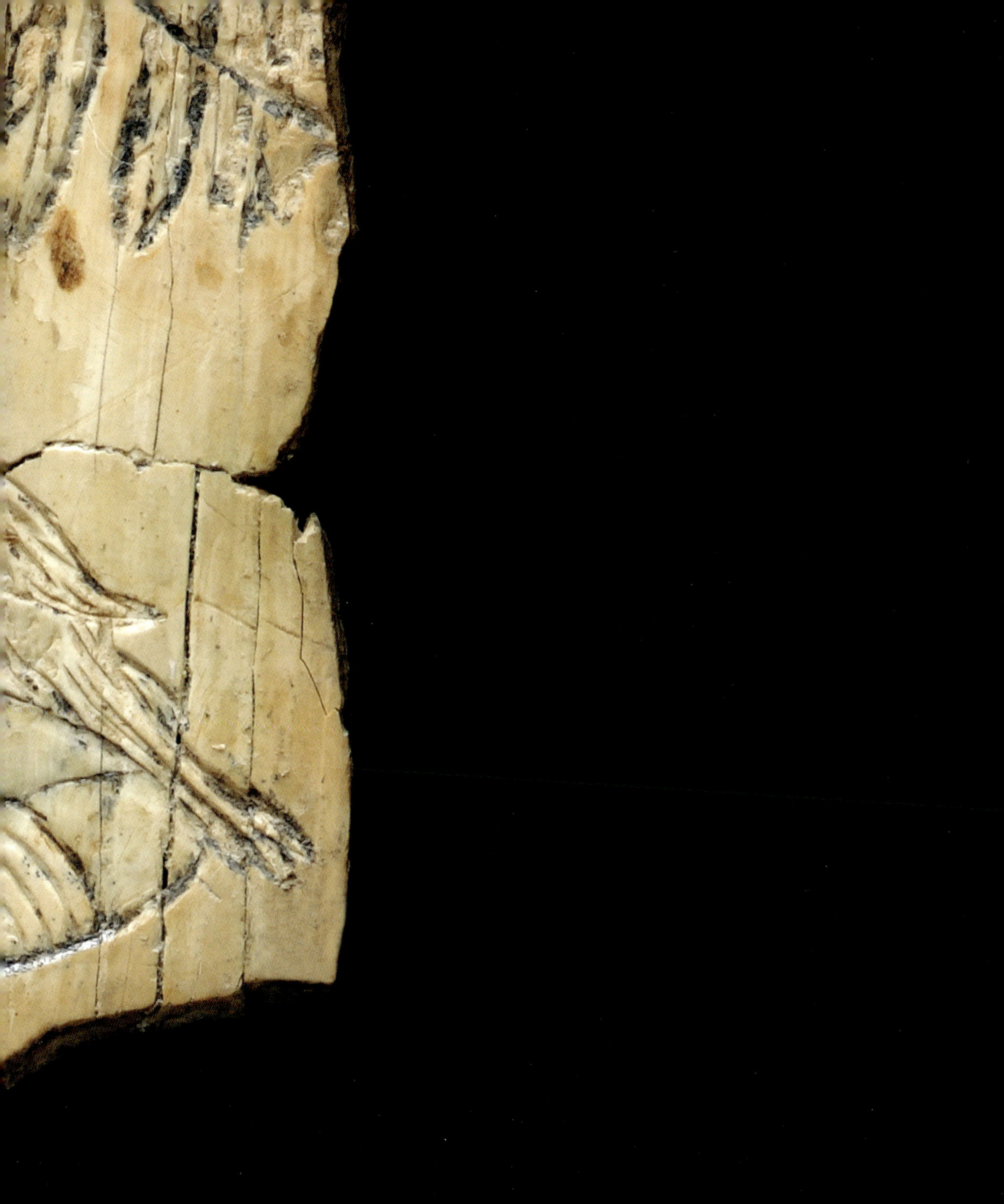

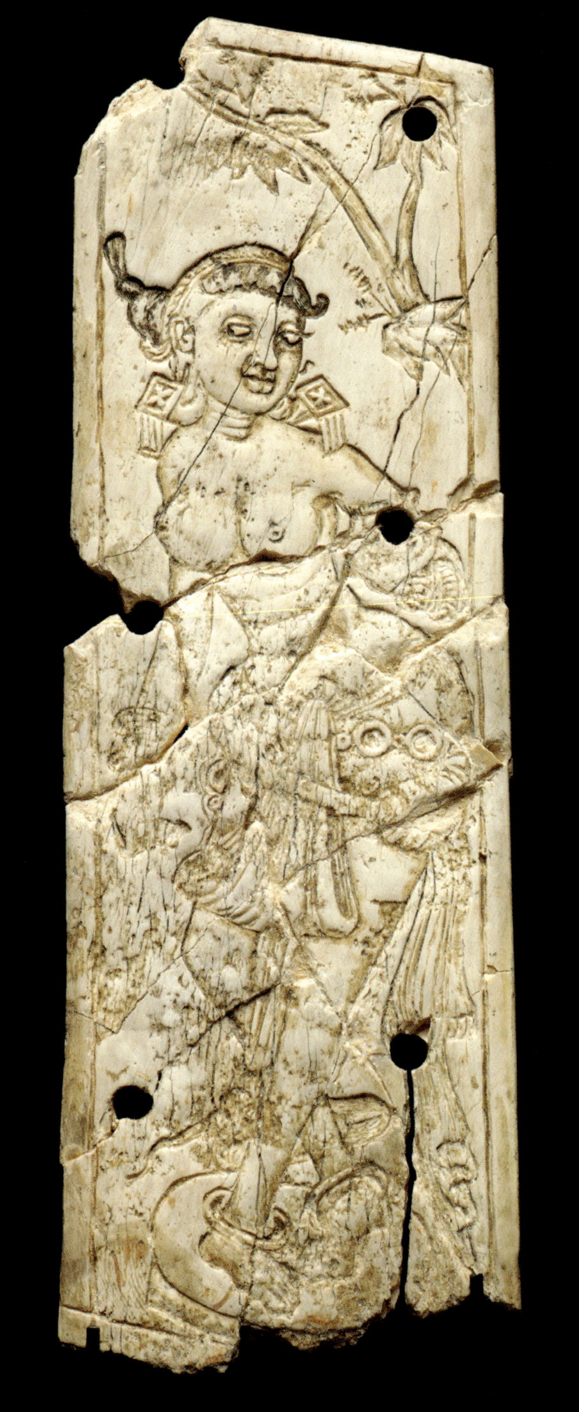

5 *Female figure pirouetting under a tree*

H 16.1 × W 5.3 × Th 0.4 cm
Room 10, Group 329, Foot Stool IX
K.p.Beg.333.73; K.M. inv. no. 58–1–60
Hackin 1939: 92, pl. LV, fig. 155; Nehru 2004: 109–10, fig. 21; Tissot 2006: 160

Incised ivory inlay showing a female figure pirouetting on a cushion with her eyes darting across in a vivacious sideways glance. The scene is set within an incised frame measuring 0.3–0.4 cm across and black pigment survives on the hair and outlines of her body. The inlay was originally attached by rivets passed through large drilled holes measuring 0.4 cm across.

Foot Stool IX was one of the most spectacular pieces of furniture found at Begram. The depiction pre-empts a later, sixth century, Indian description of the auspicious signs epitomizing female beauty: 'Broad, plump and heavy hips to support the girdle, and navel deep, large and turned to the right, a middle with three folds and not hairy; breasts round, close to each other, equal and hard … and neck marked with three lines, bring wealth and joy' (*Brihatsamhitā* by Varāhamihira). The woman is wearing a pair of anklets, a very distinctive pair of heavy decorated earrings with triple drops, and a decorated bow. Her hair is pulled into a wavy fringe at the front and knotted behind into a projecting ponytail. One scholar has suggested the bow is in fact a ribbon and that as this feature is unparalleled in Indian art this might imply local manufacture for this piece. Extensive black pigment survives on the hair.

The figure is topless but is wearing a cloth around her waist secured with a distinctive type of hip girdle decorated with roundels, perhaps representing semi-precious stone settings held together with large chain links. Many of the women shown on these inlays are wearing broad hip girdles: some of these are shown as made up of three separate strands of beadwork, others appear to be sashes but this one is more elaborate still. A market for such items is referred to in the first century account, the *Periplus*, which lists 'multicoloured girdles, eighteen inches wide' among goods sold at the north-west Indian port of Barygaza (*Periplus* 49, transl. Casson 1989: 81).

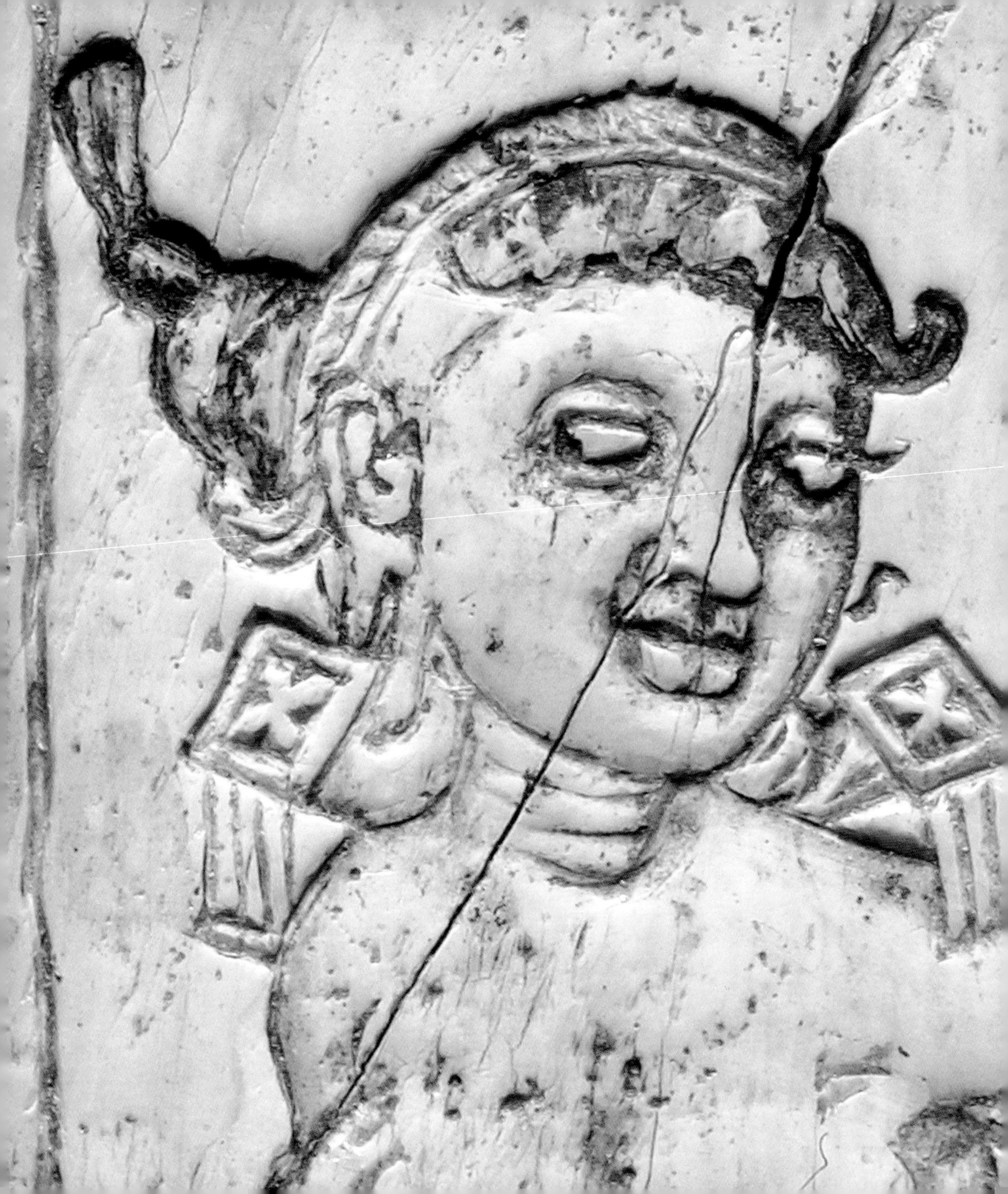

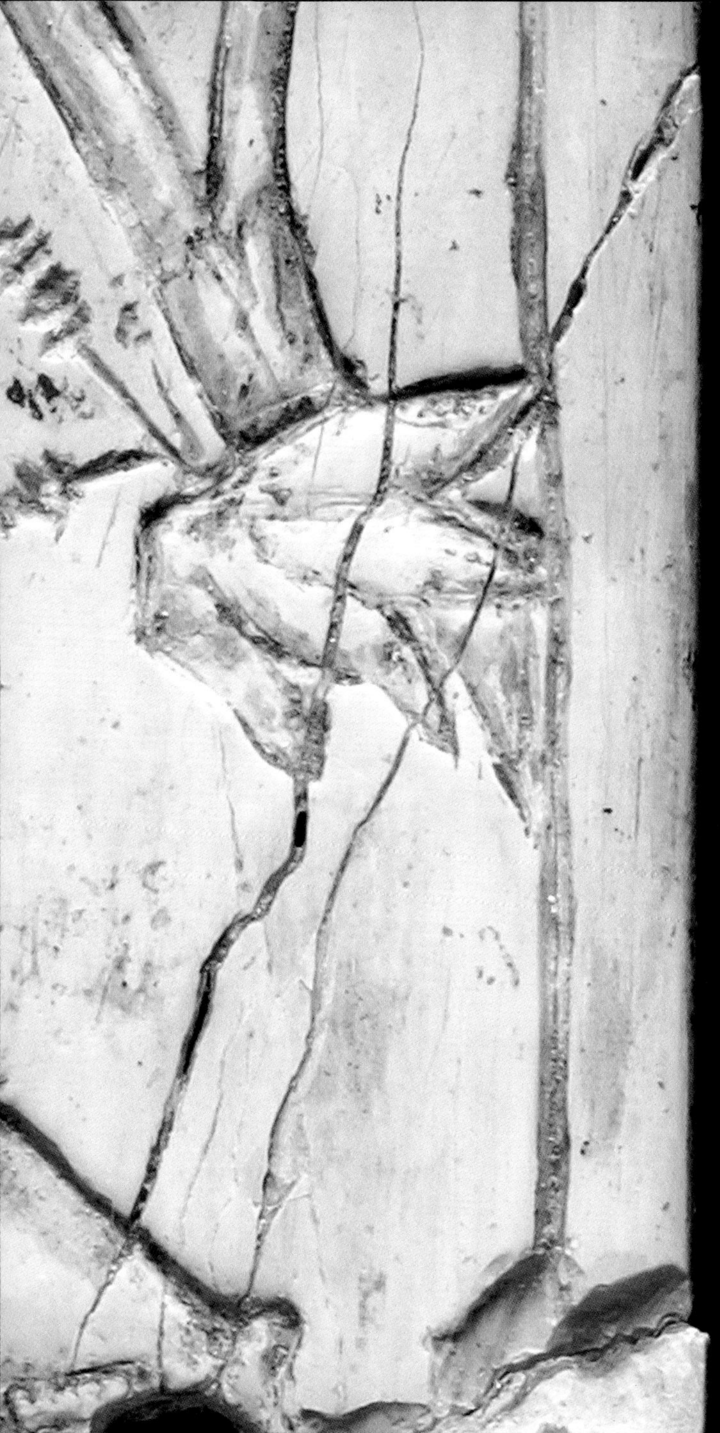

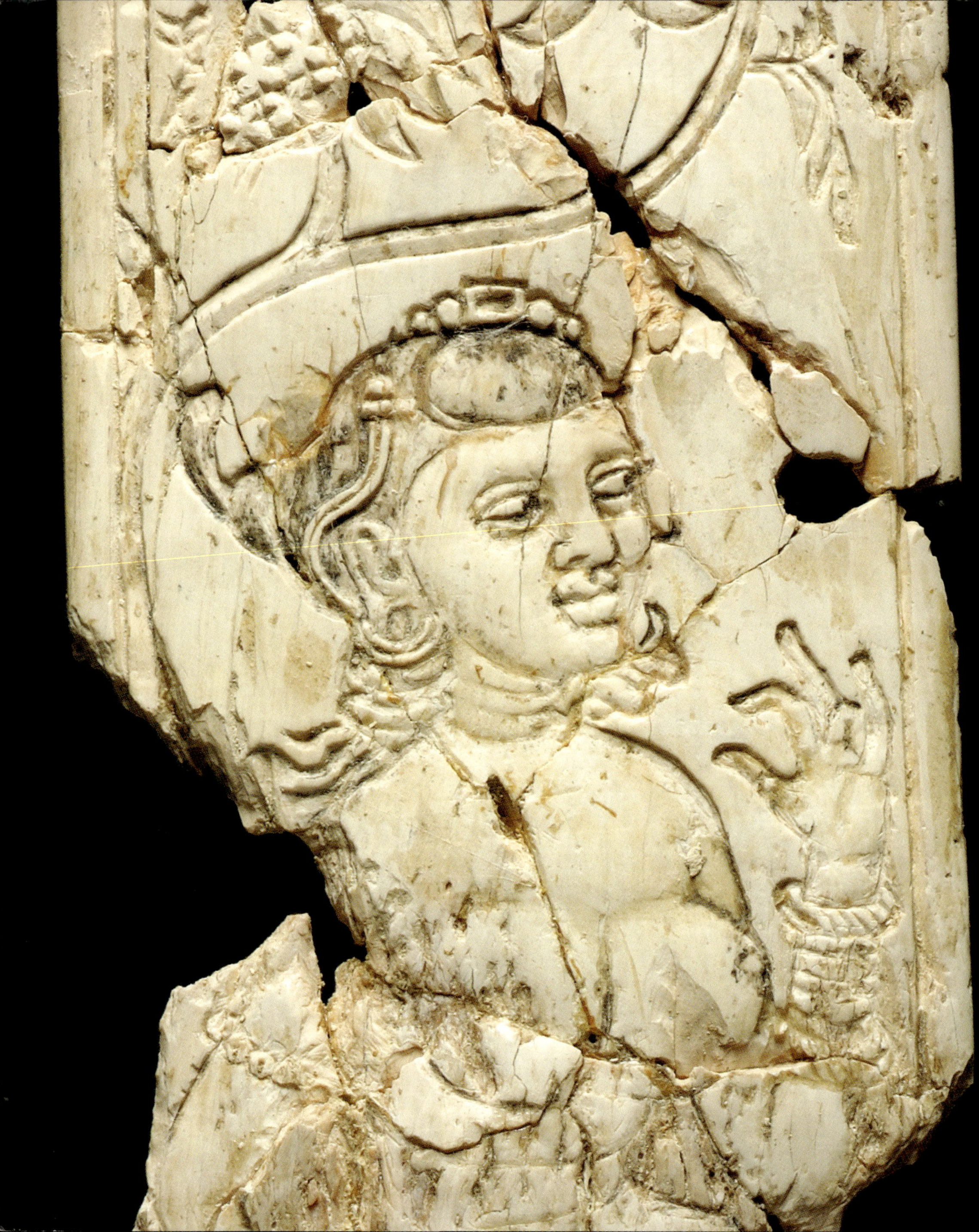

6 *Female figure beneath a tree*

H 16.8 × W 5.1–5.2 × Th 0.2 cm
Room 10, Group 329, Foot Stool IX
Previously unpublished

Incised ivory inlay showing a female figure beneath
a curving branch bearing fruit. Extensive traces
of black pigment survive on the incised outlines,
details of the body and her hair which is pulled
into a knotted ponytail with a decorative bow on
the top of her head. She is wearing earrings, twisted
bangles and a cloth girdle similar to that worn in
inlay **5**. Her left hand is raised and fingers bent as
the carver captures her in an elegant dance move.
The figure is set within an incised outer frame or
border 0.3 cm wide and was originally attached to
a piece of furniture using rivets passed through
the holes, which measure 0.4 cm across.

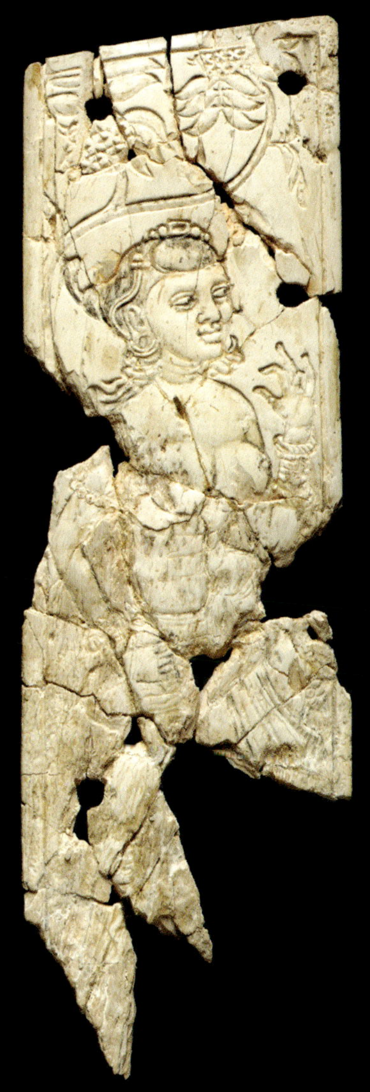

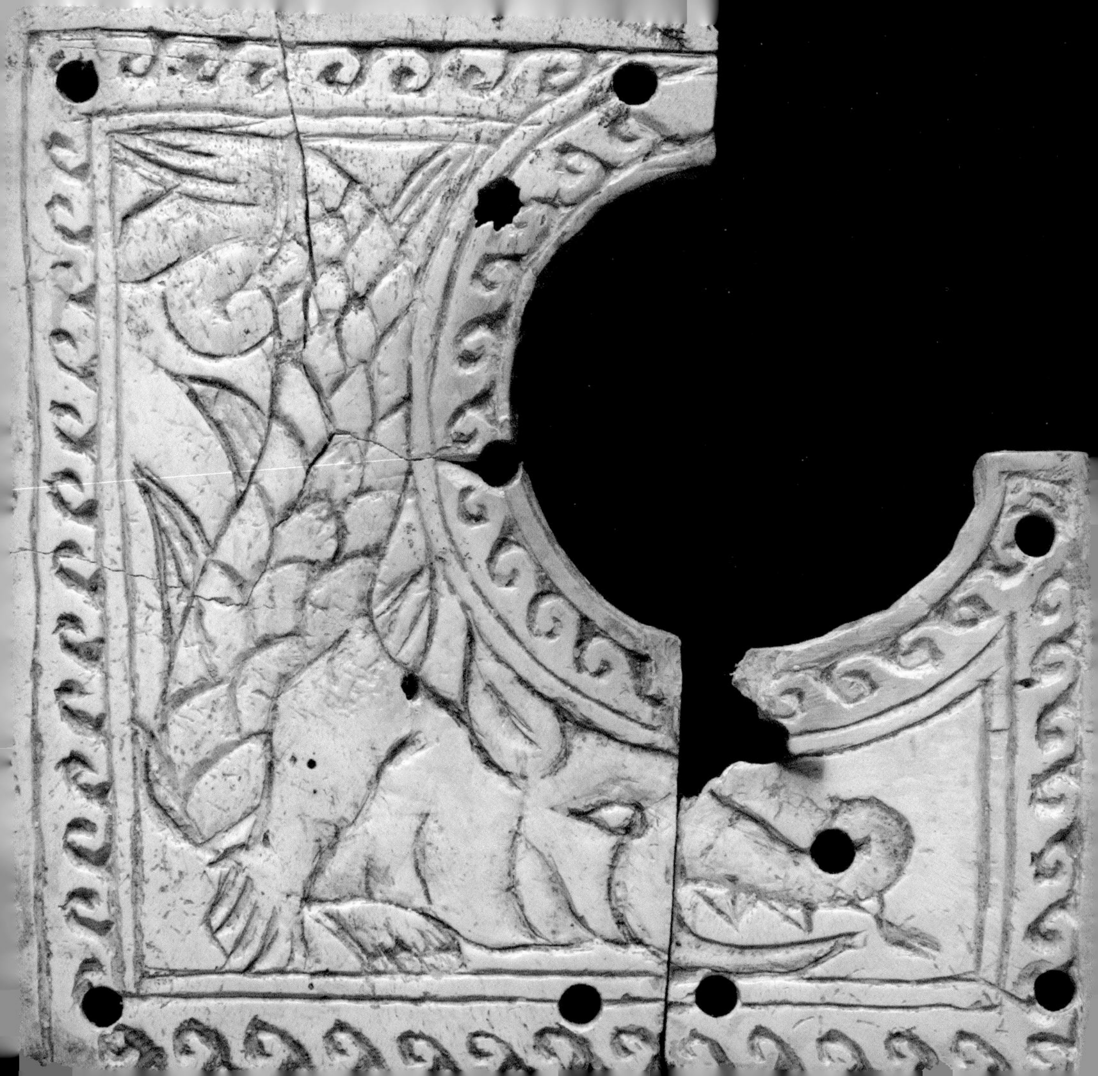

7 *Makara*

H 8.7 × W 9.0 × Th 0.3 cm
Room 10, Group 325, Foot Stool V
K.p.Beg.312.52; K.M. inv. no. 59–1–4
Hackin 1939: 79, pl. L, fig. 131; Tissot 2006: 154

Incised ivory inlay made up of two almost rectangular strips showing
a *makara*, a mythological creature combining parts of an elephant,
crocodile and fish, framed within a decorative border. It was originally
secured with rivets fixed through the small circular holes around the
edges that measure 0.3 cm across. Traces of dark pigment survive in
the incised areas, particularly on the beast itself.

8 *Bird walking to the left*

H 8.9 × W 9.2 × Th 0.3 cm
Room 10, Group 325, Foot Stool V
K.p.Beg.306.46; K.M. inv. no. 59–1–1
Hackin 1939: 78, pl. XLIX, fig. 127; Tissot 2006: 152

Incised ivory inlay made up of three strips showing a duck walking left within a decorative border. It was originally secured with rivets passed through the circular holes around the edge, which measure 0.3 cm across. Traces of dark pigment survive in the incised areas.

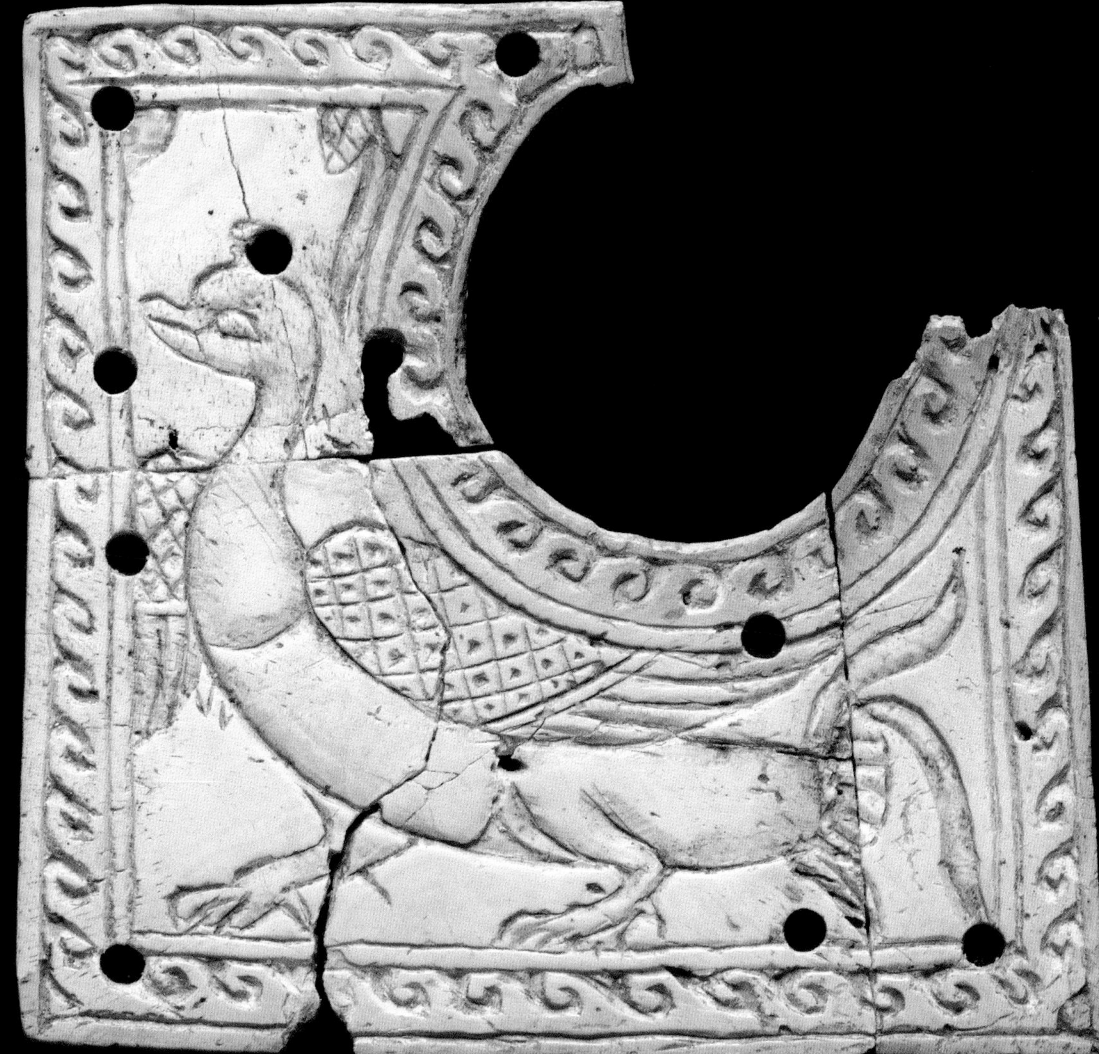

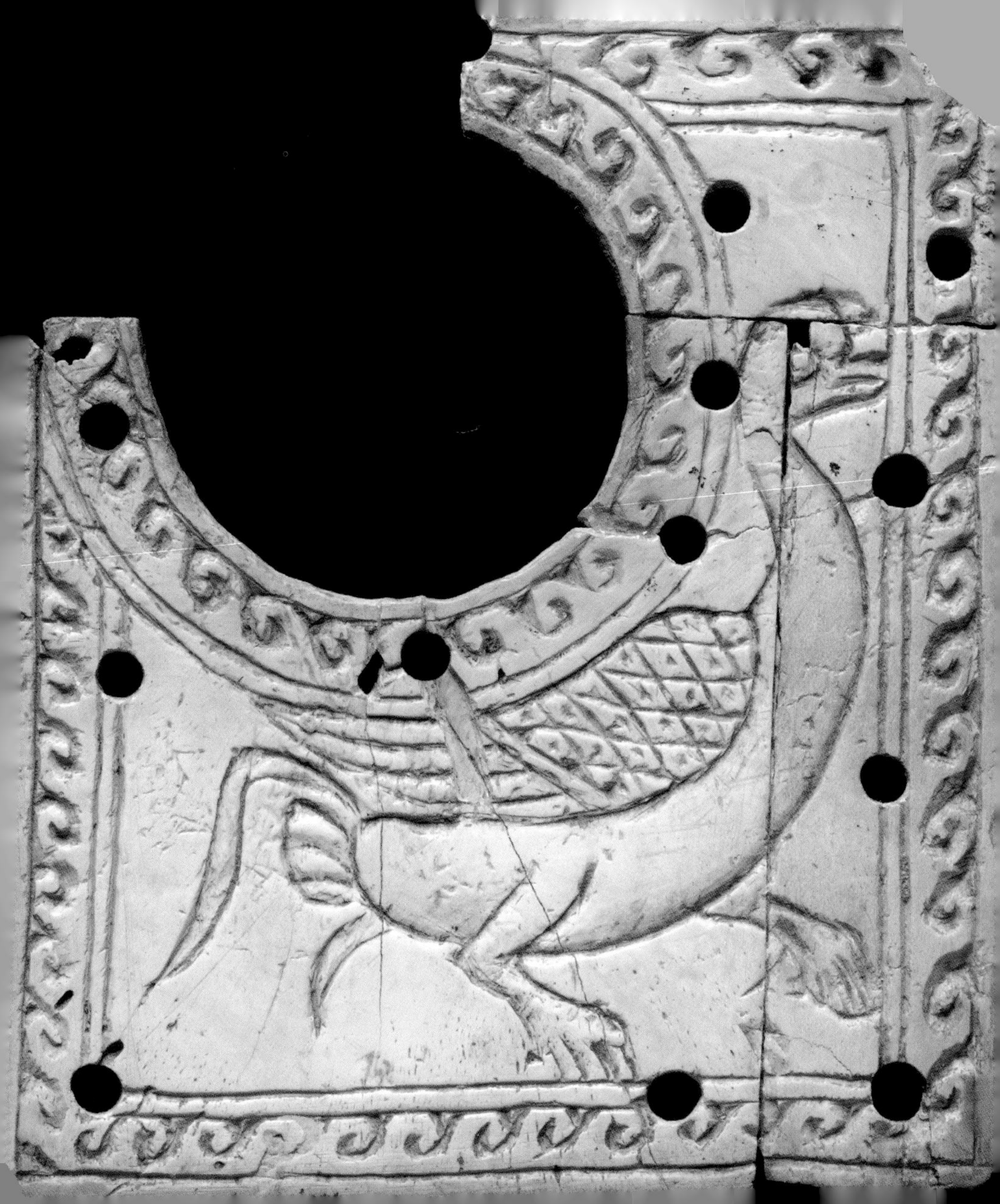

incised ivory inlay made up of three strips showing a duck walking
right within a decorative border. It was originally secured with rivets
passed through the circular holes around the edge, which measure
0.3 cm across. Traces of dark pigment survive in the incised outlines
and feathers of the bird.

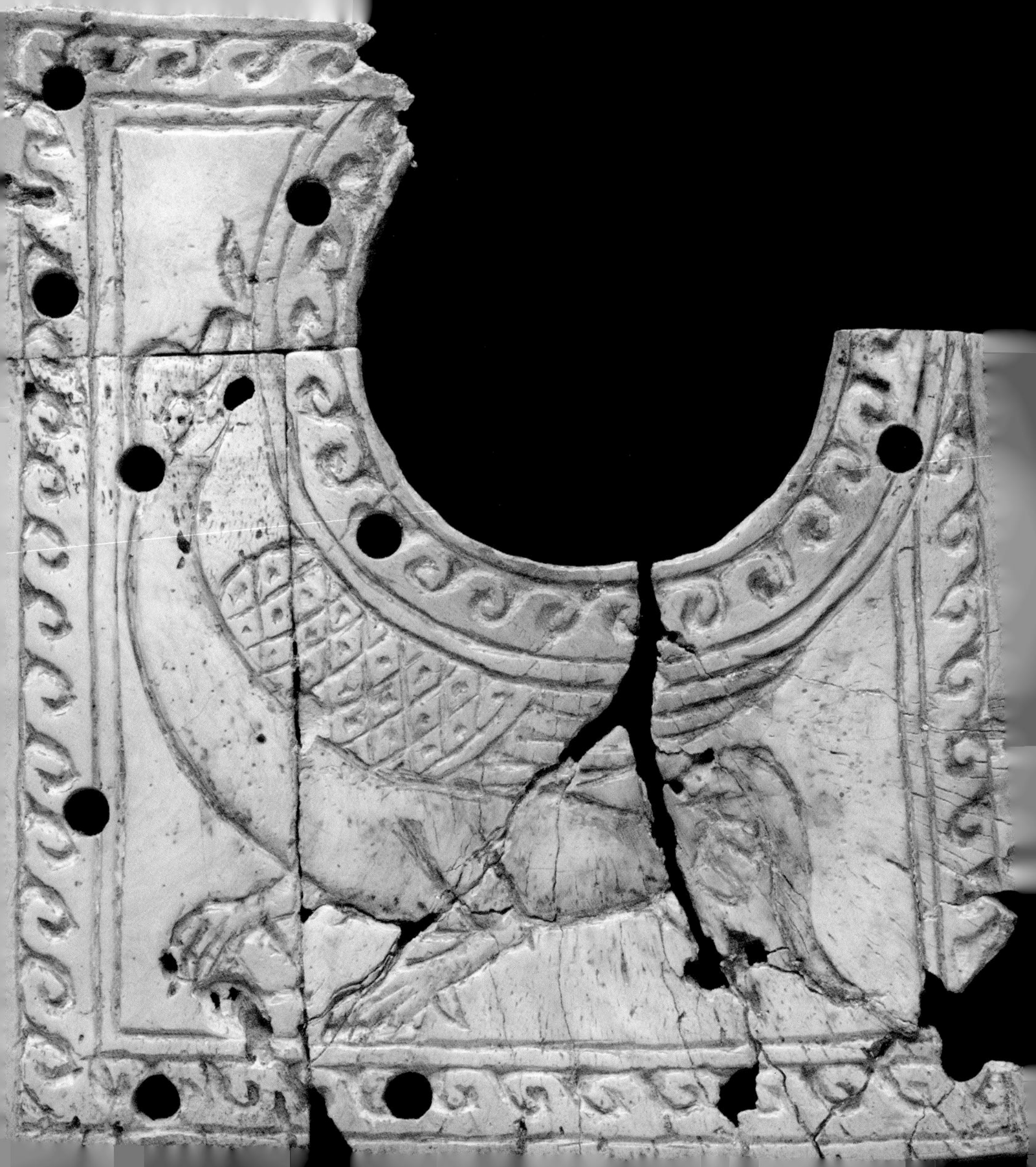

10 *Bird walking to the left with its head turned*

H 9.1 × W 8.3 × Th 0.3 cm
Room 10, Group 325, Foot Stool V
Previously unpublished

Incised ivory inlay made up of three strips showing a duck walking
left with its head raised and set within a decorative border. It was
originally secured with rivets passed through the circular holes around
the edge, which measure 0.3 cm across. There are traces of dark
pigment in the incised areas.

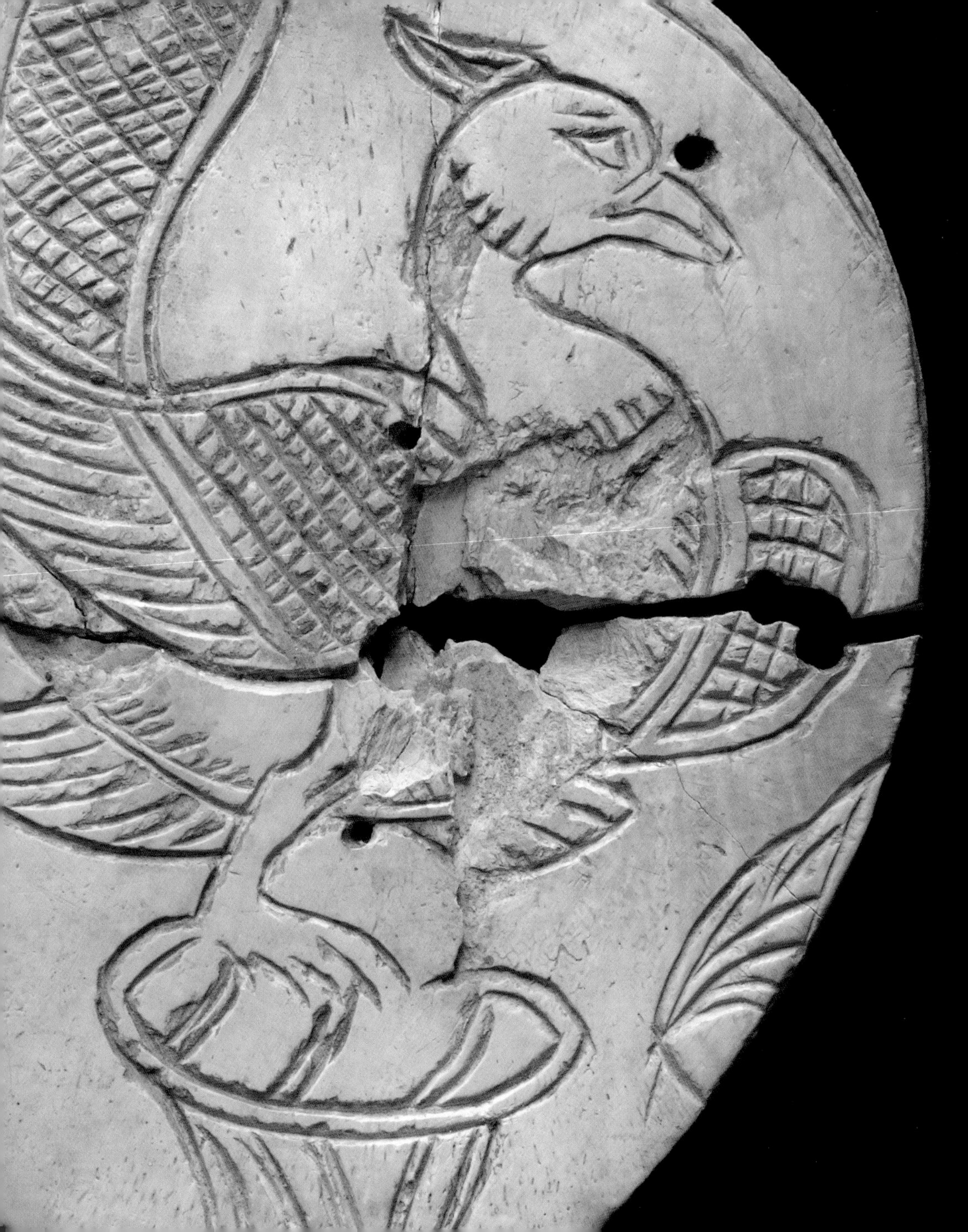

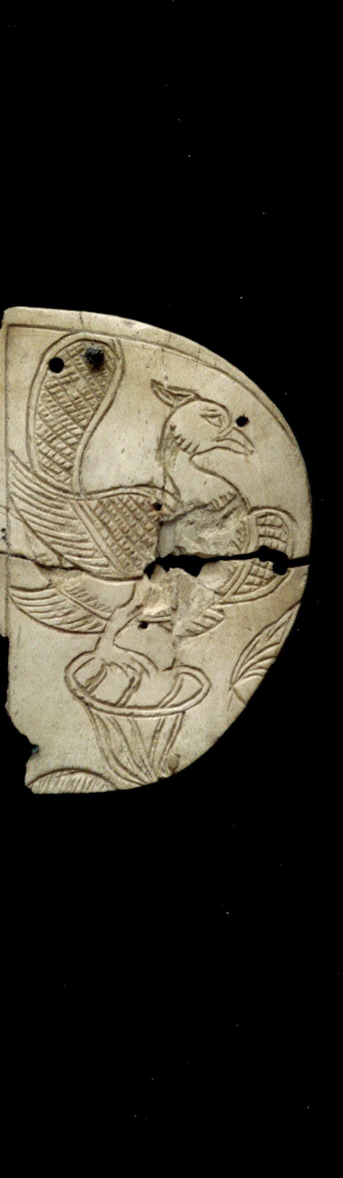

 Crested bird standing on a lotus

H 8.4 × W 5.6 × Th 0.3 cm
Room 10, Group 321, Foot Stool I
K.p.Beg.285.25; K.M. inv. no. 59–1–5
Hackin 1939: 69, pl. XLII, fig. 92; Nehru 2004: 105, fig. 8; Tissot 2006: 145

Incised ivory inlay showing a crested bird standing on a lotus and facing right. Extensive traces of red pigment (identified as vermilion) survive on the wing feathers whereas black pigment was used to highlight the incised outline of the bird. The centre of the inlay is pierced by two small holes, 0.1 cm across; a series of irregularly spaced larger holes at the top and bottom were used to secure the inlay in place and two of these still retain copper alloy rivets: the better preserved of these measures only 0.7 cm long, has a rounded head, 0.3 cm across, and a pointed tip.

The economic use of line combined with the spirited style of this piece, along with other bone inlays found together as Group 321 and depicting a variety of other birds in movement or alighting, have led one scholar to suggest these were products of a school of bone carving centred in Bactria rather than India. The few parallels are not convincing, however, and their place of origin remains open. Moreover, the material of this inlay is ivory.

12 *Playful lion*

H 6.9 × W 4.5–5.1 × Th 0.4 cm
Room 10, Group 329, Foot Stool IX
K.p.Beg.335.75; K.M. inv. no. 58–1–54
Hackin 1939: 94, pl. LVI, fig. 167; Tissot 2006: 160

Incised and slightly trapezoidal ivory panel showing a lion with its head and body partly turned. There are traces of black pigment in the incised outlines and borders. The design is framed by a single incised line, above and below which there are some areas of loss and brownish staining. This piece has suffered particularly since it was excavated and first published.

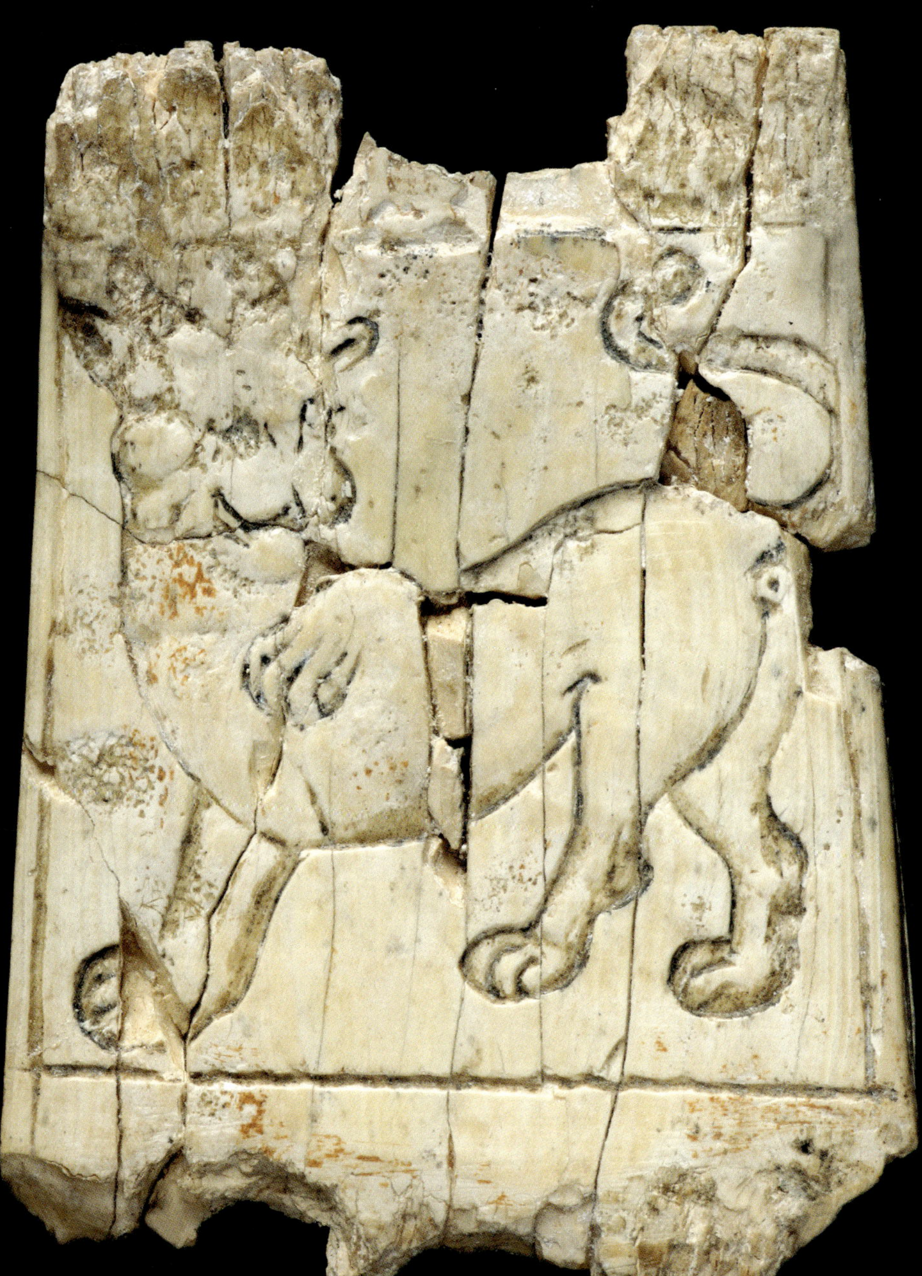

13 *Seated figure with a feathered crown*

H 9.4 × W 5.2 × Th 0.3 cm
Room 13, Chair 2
K.p.Beg.457.197; K.M. inv. no. 58–1–213
Hackin 1954: 237, fig. 192, no. 207; Tissot 2006: 207

Incised bone inlay showing a squatting *yaksha*,
a winged tree spirit who was worshipped as a
guardian of hidden mineral treasures. This figure
was therefore associated with wealth and abundance
and was a male counterpart to the *yakshi*. The figure
has his hands on his hips and is wearing a plumed
headdress. The decoration above shows the splayed
feet of a vase which, continued on a separate plaque,
was filled with flowers. The extensive traces of red
pigment on the background have been identified as
vermilion. This piece originally decorated the lower
section of a foot of Chair 2.

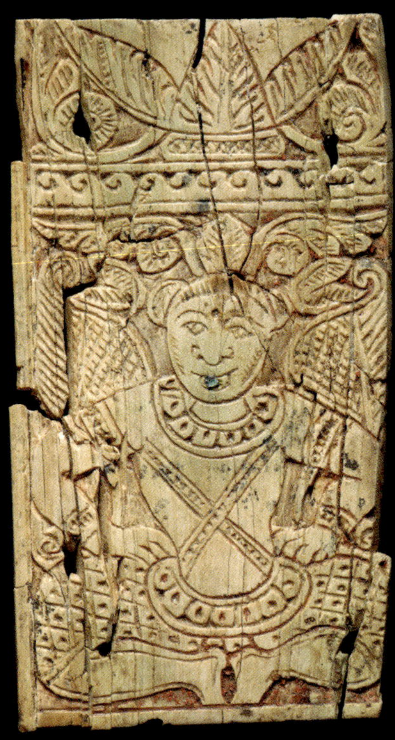

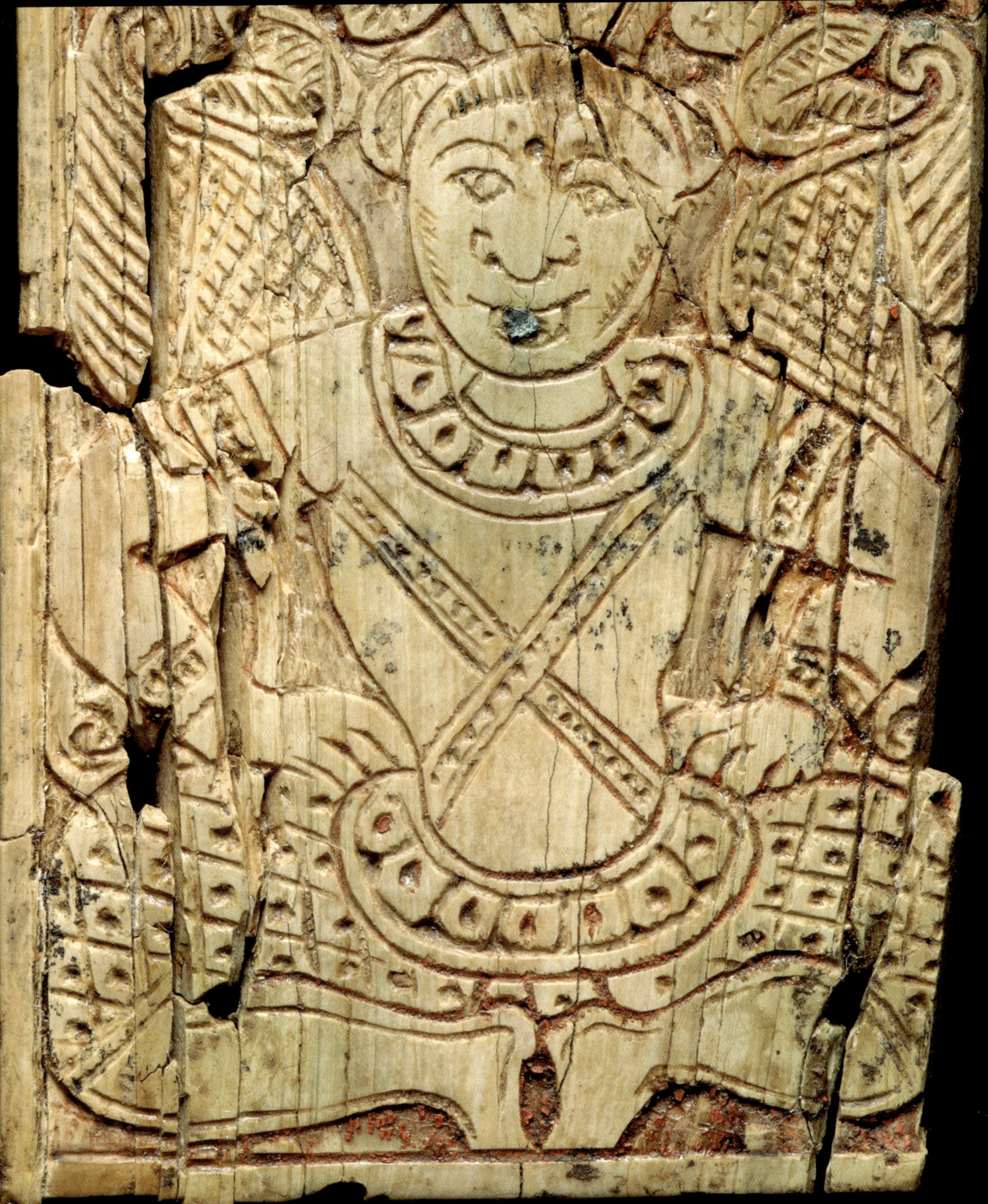

14 *Lions and elephant*

H 6.5 × W 6.1 × Th 0.3 cm (left); H 6.5 × W 6.9–7.1 × Th 0.3 cm (right)
Room 13, Chair 3
K.p.Beg.542.282; K.M. inv. no. 58–1–240
Hackin 1954: 202, fig. 189, no. 150w. *5 ter.*; Tissot 2006: 230

These two openwork plaques are carved from ivory.
One shows a pair of lions, the other shows an Indian
elephant ambling right with its trunk partially
coiled. Both are framed within squashed roundels
linked on either side with additional roundels
carved as separate plaques. The plain borders at the
top and bottom help to emphasize the linear nature
of the scenes and would have enabled the plaques
to be attached within runnels and each secured
in place with four small copper alloy pins passed
through holes in the roundel borders.

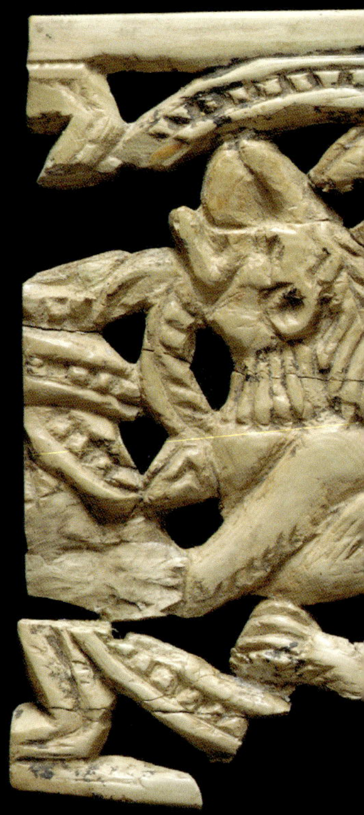

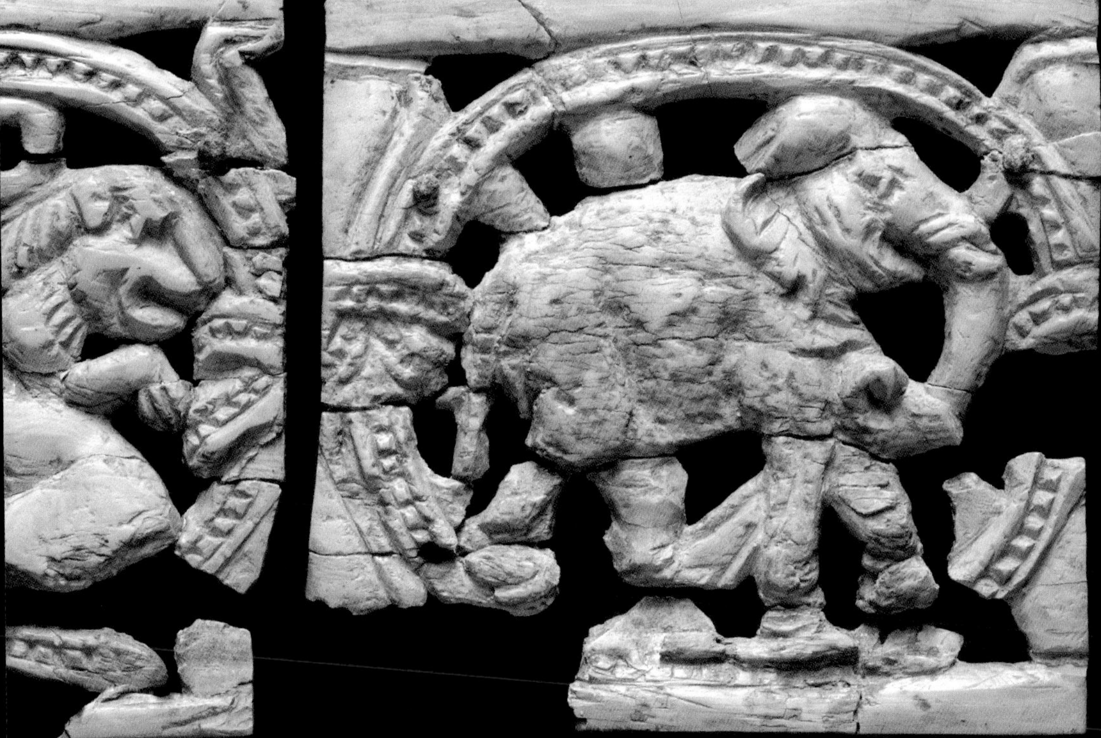

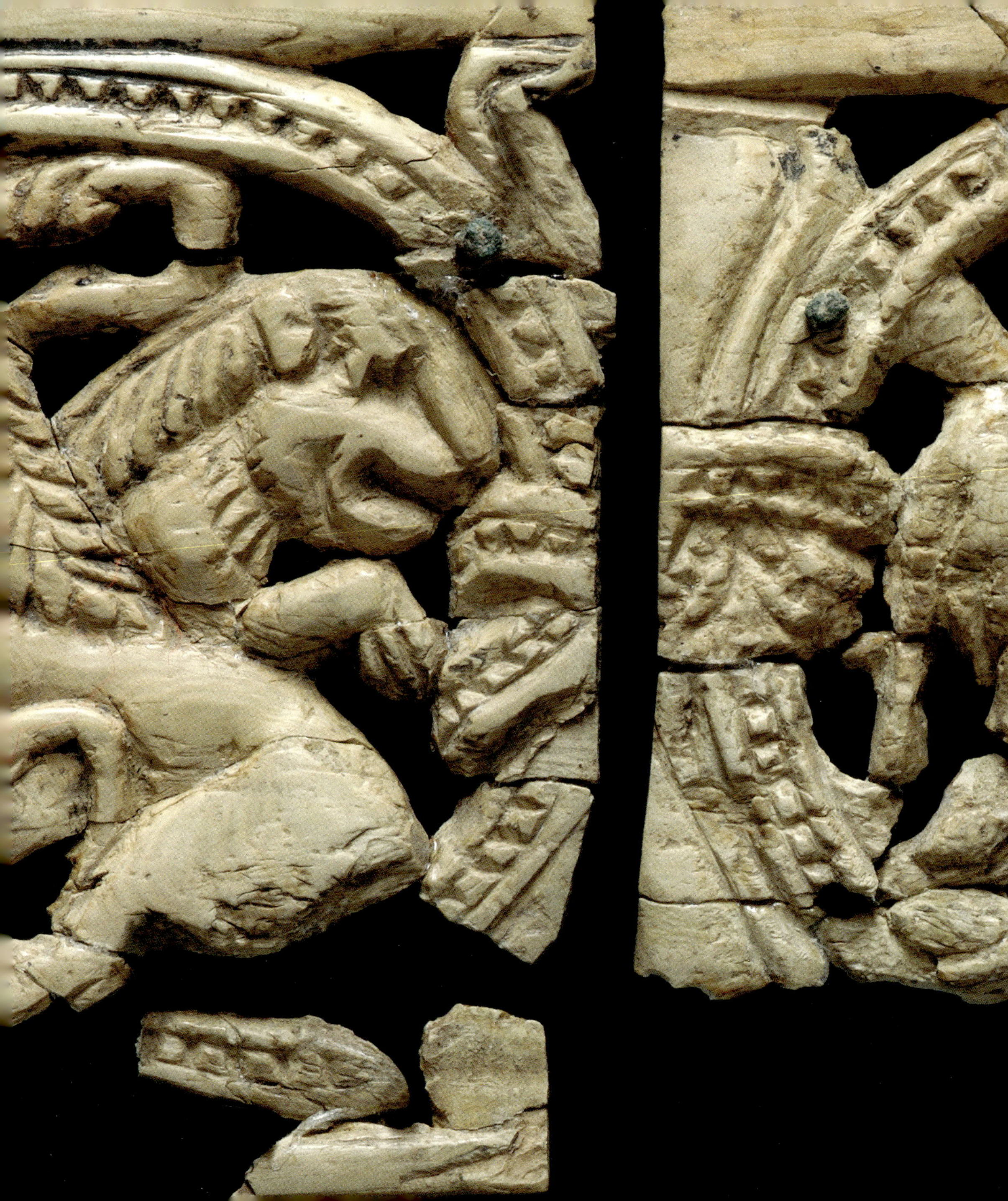

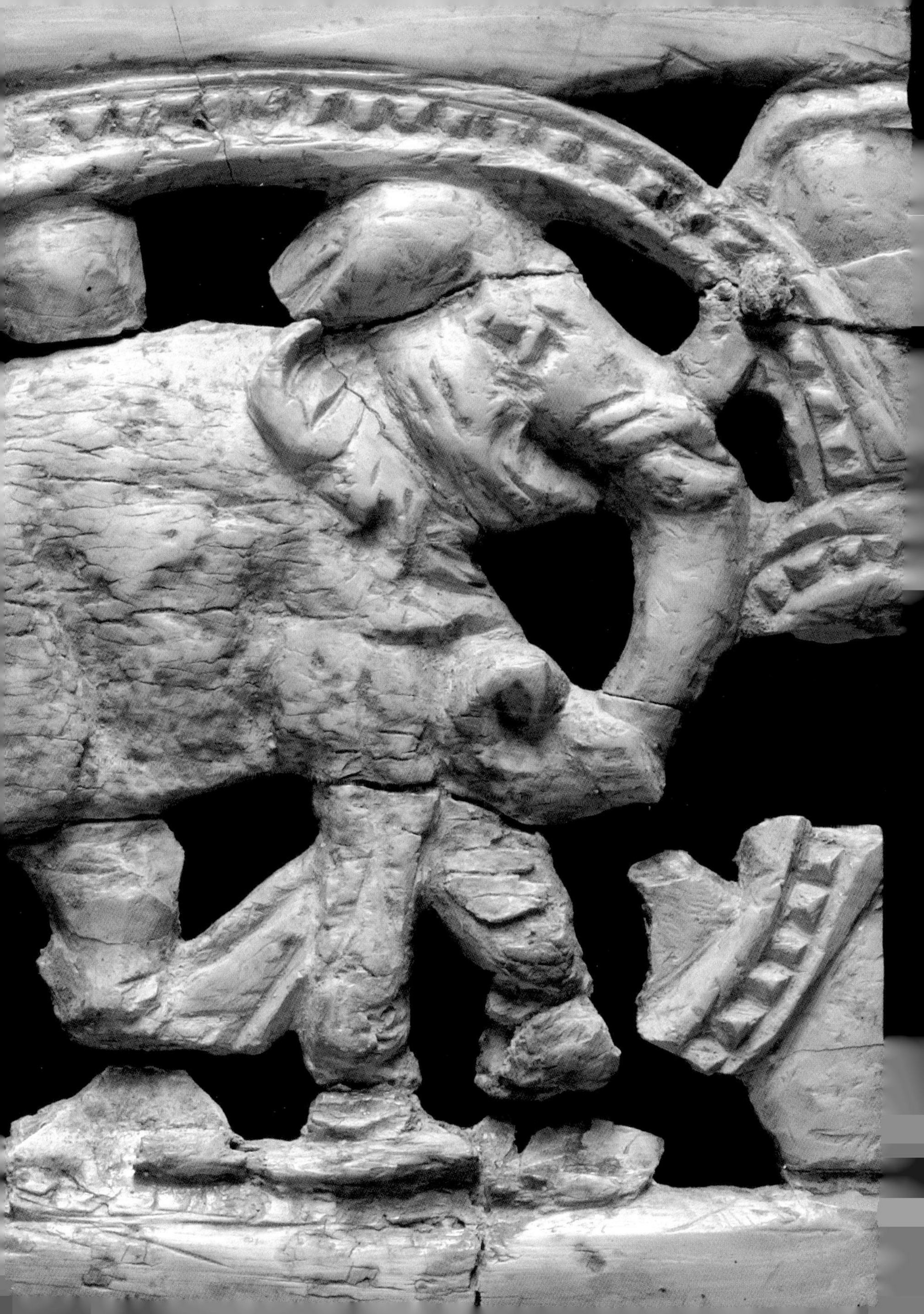

15 *Elephant and riders*

H 8.7 × W 11.9 × Th 2.2 cm
Room 13
K.p.Beg.596.336; K.M. inv. no. 58–1–166
Tissot 2006: 244

This badly weathered openwork ivory plaque
shows a kneeling elephant facing right and
carrying three women on its back, who face
the viewer. A fourth woman stands at the rear.
Small copper alloy pins were passed through
the corners of the main inlay plaque and two
additional pins used to secure the separate
carved inlay strip along the top.

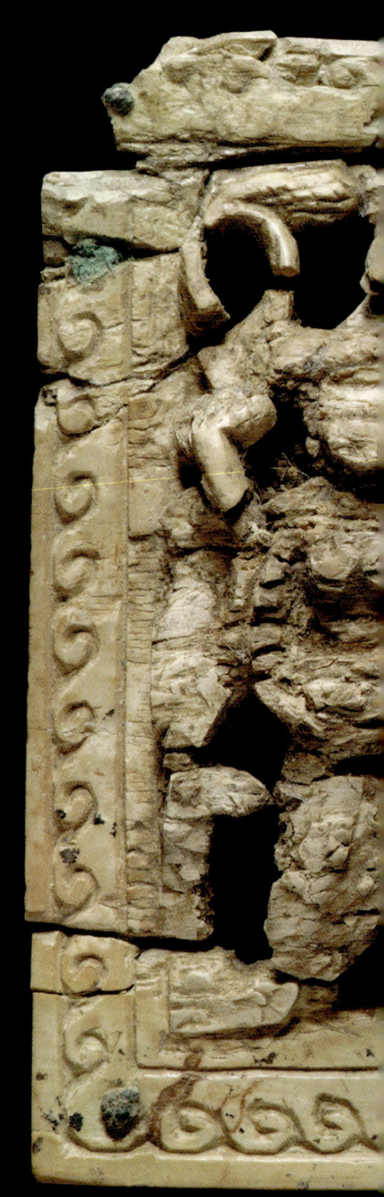

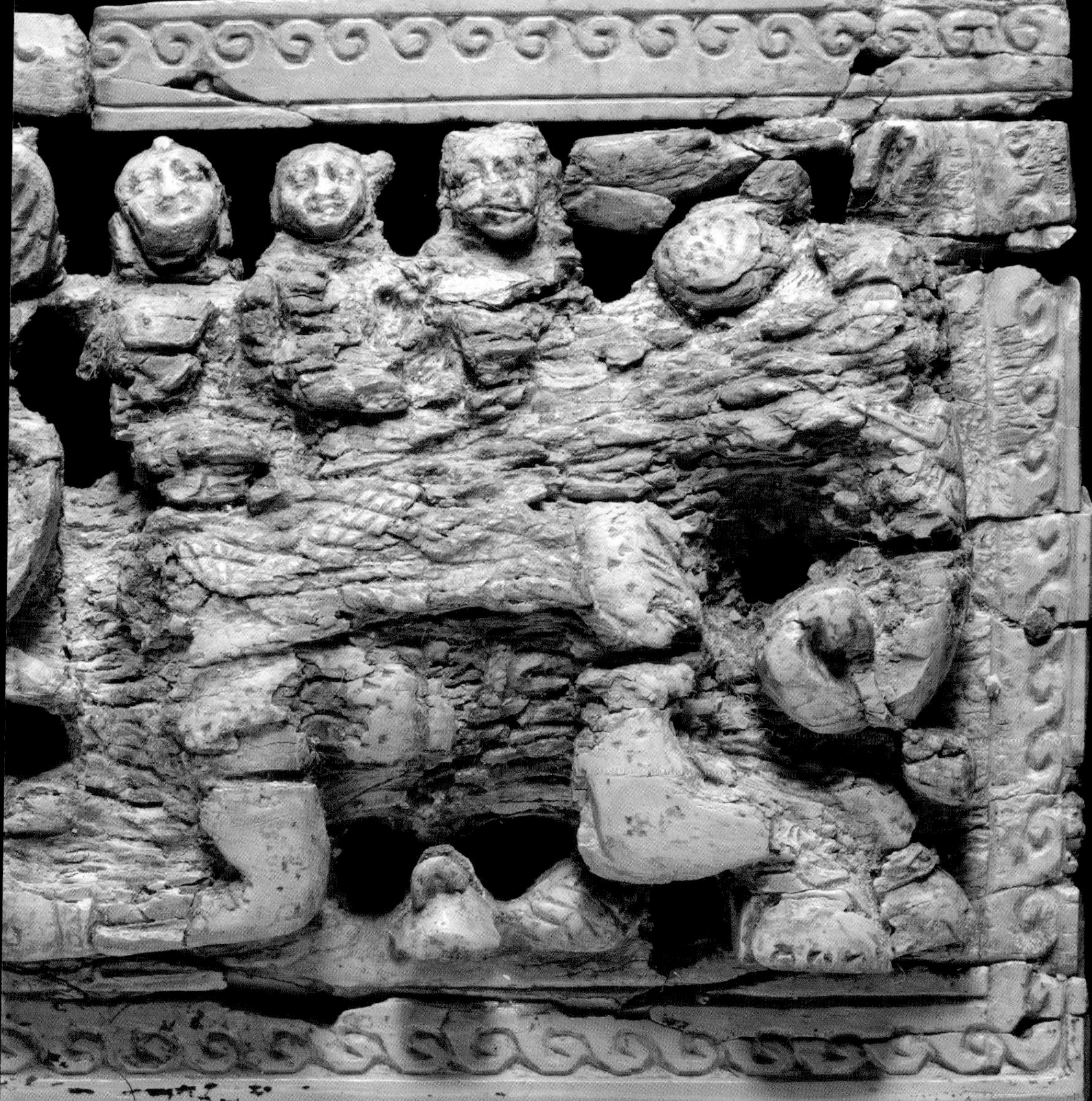

16 *Mythical creatures with riders*

H 5.3 × W 19.6 × Th 0.3 cm
Room 10, Group 327
Hackin 1954: fig. 236, no. XII

This very fragmentary ivory inlay was part of an openwork frieze showing nude
women wearing beaded hip girdles riding mythical beasts and controlling them
through the reins. Two other figures are standing near the centre, holding spears
and framing a larger figure facing the viewer and wearing a V-necked garment.
The inlay was secured with copper alloy rivets 0.2 cm across. It was found with
a large number of other, equally fragmentary, pieces but it has not yet been
possible to reconstruct the original appearance of the whole composition.

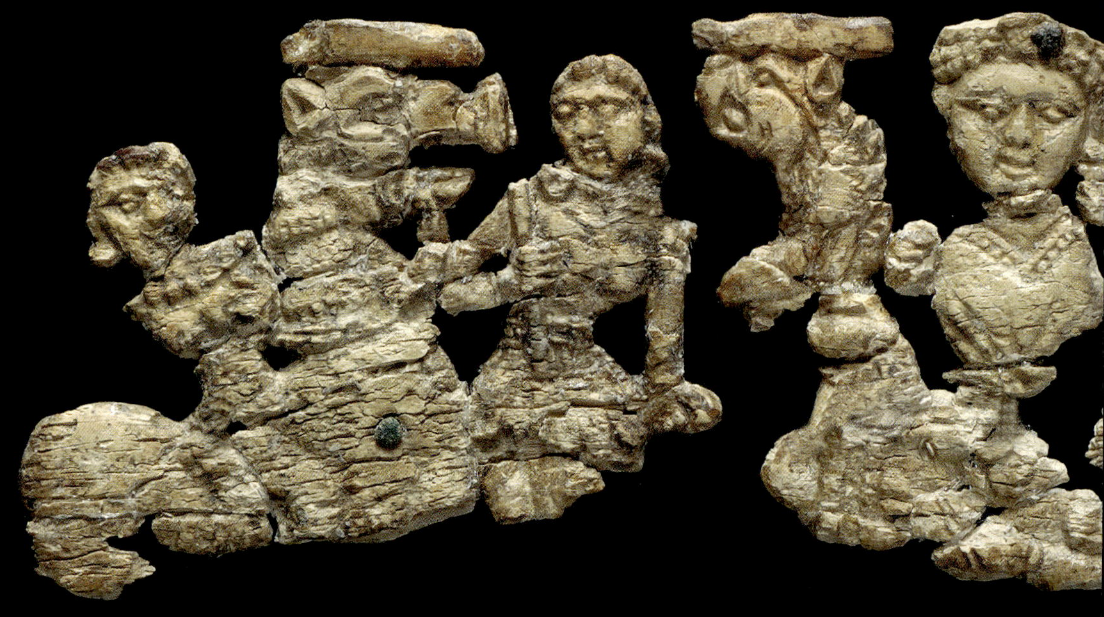

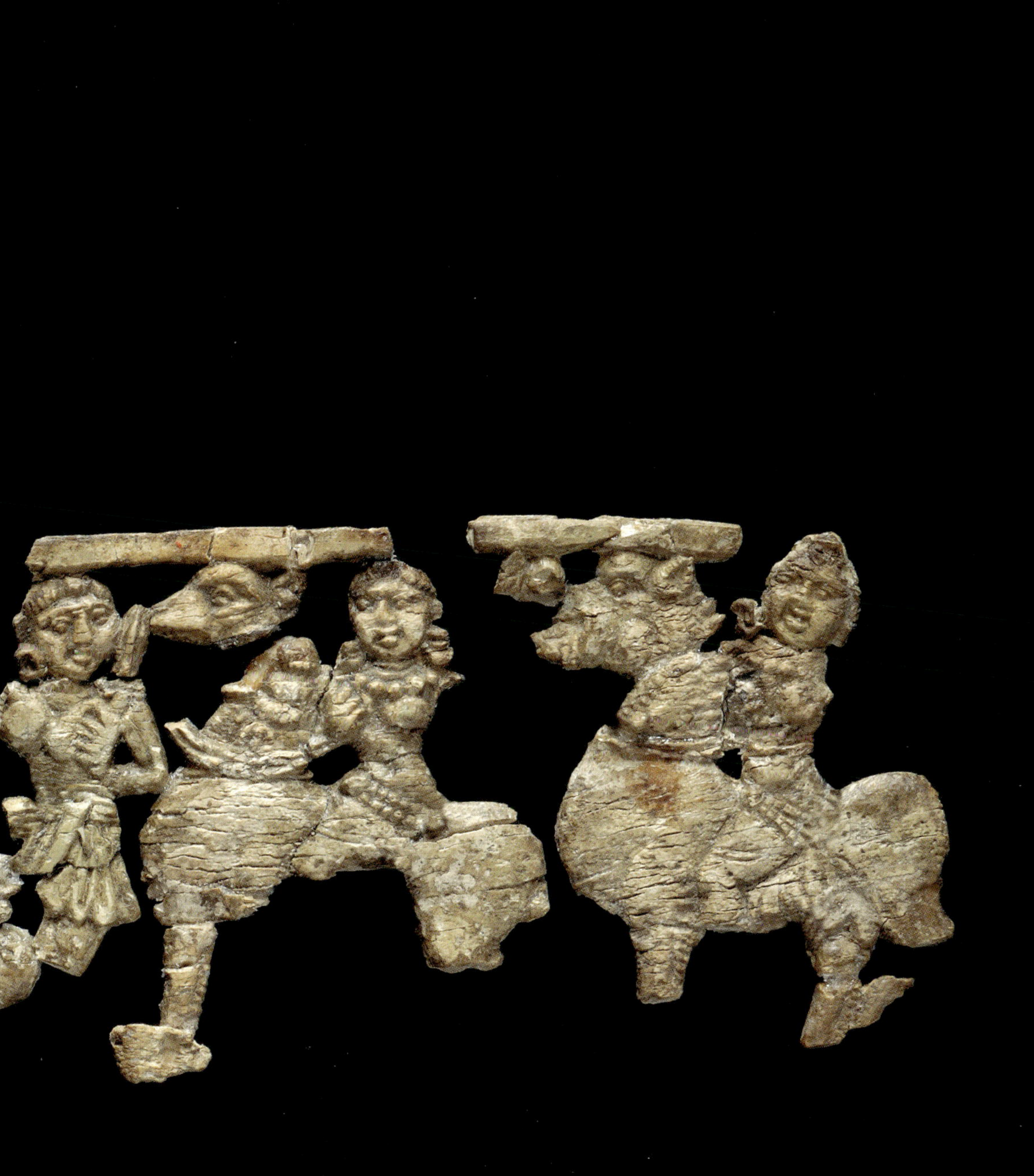

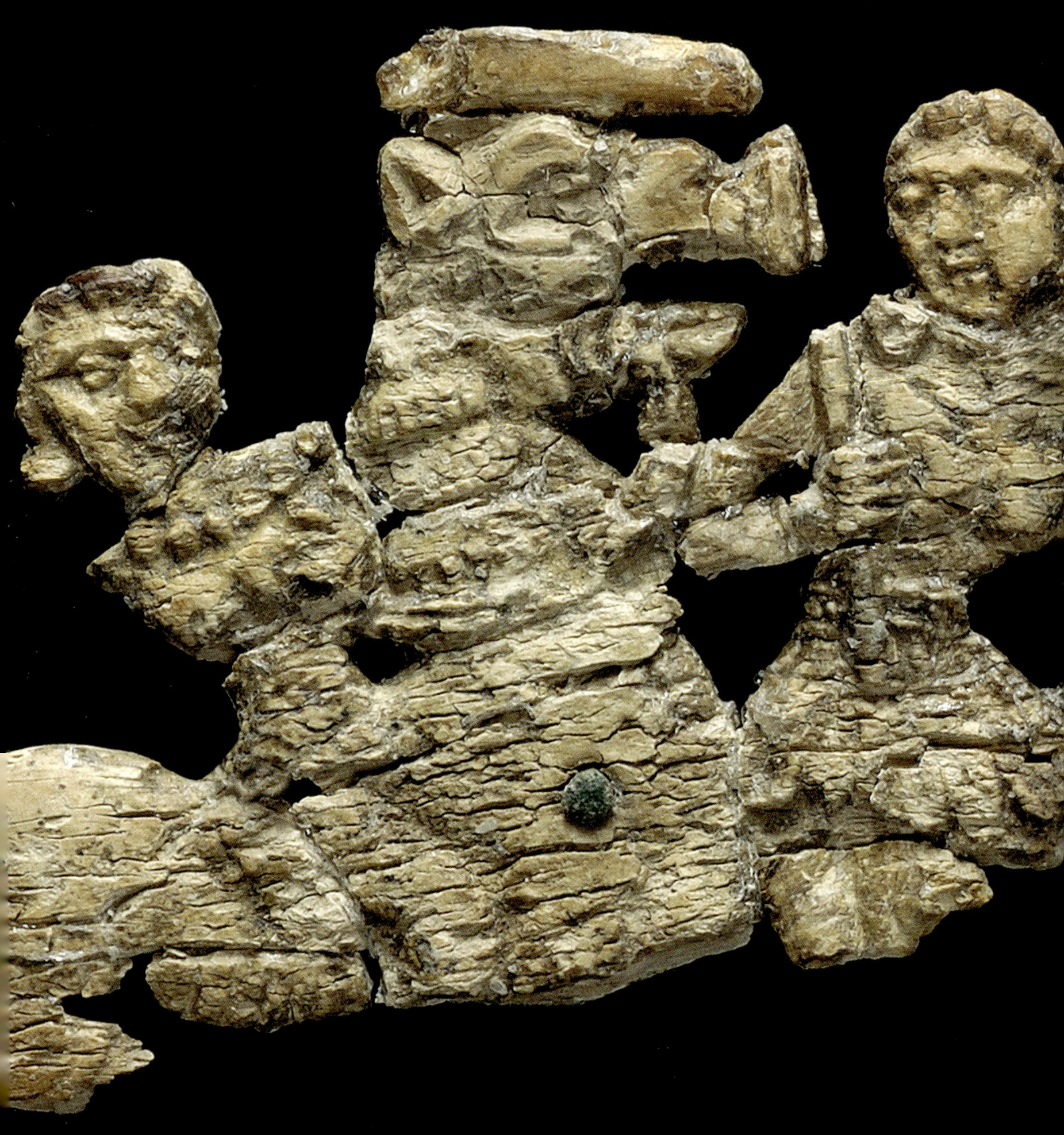

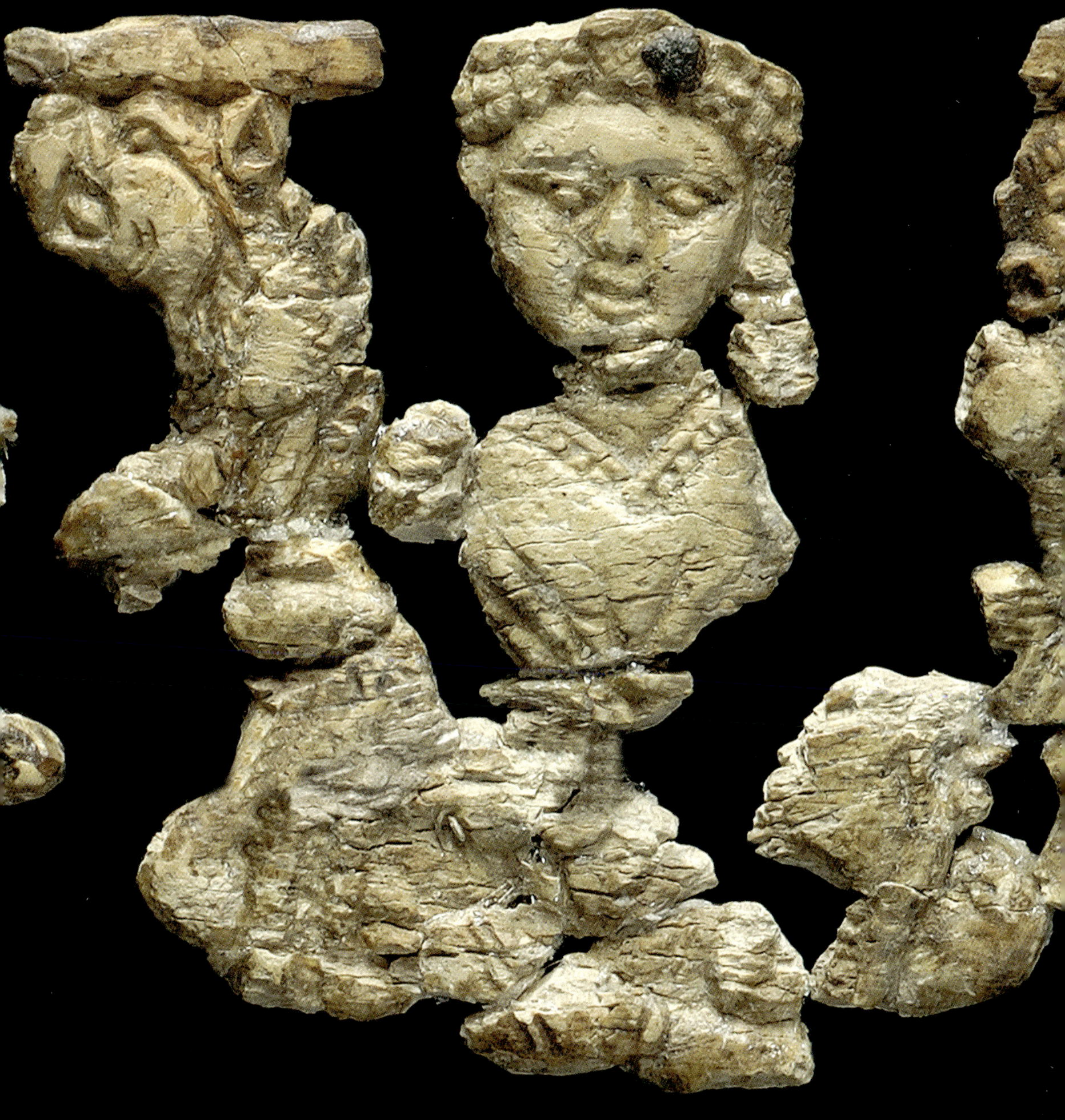

This openwork ivory inlay was originally part of a chair. It was found in a very fragmentary state and further parts have been lost since its original discovery and publication. It belonged to either Chair 1 or 4, found piled on top of one another. It was originally secured with copper alloy rivets, of which one remains passed through the centre of a red coloured quatrefoil in the lower border.

The female figures wear multiple bangles on each forearm, heavy decorated anklets and loose flowing trousers secured with beaded hip girdles. The style of carving of the trousers resembles depictions on later cave paintings at Ajantā in western India that were interpreted as evidence of dyed ikats. At least two of these women also appear to be wearing a broad beaded necklace and are topless. Their hair is plaited in a different manner from the women in the inlays discussed above and they are depicted with different items of furniture, a folding table and a low couch supported on geometric turned legs, probably of wood or ivory.

Extensive traces of pigment survive on the quatrefoil petals which form the bottom border. These are coloured alternately red and blue with vermilion and indigo. This four-petalled design is a very ancient Indian motif beginning in Harappan times but it also occurs as the border to a narrative scene on a carved ivory found at Kondapur, a Satavahana site in Andhra Pradesh, and on an ivory spacer bead with a duck design found at Śiśupālgarh near Bubaneswar, both dated to the first or second centuries

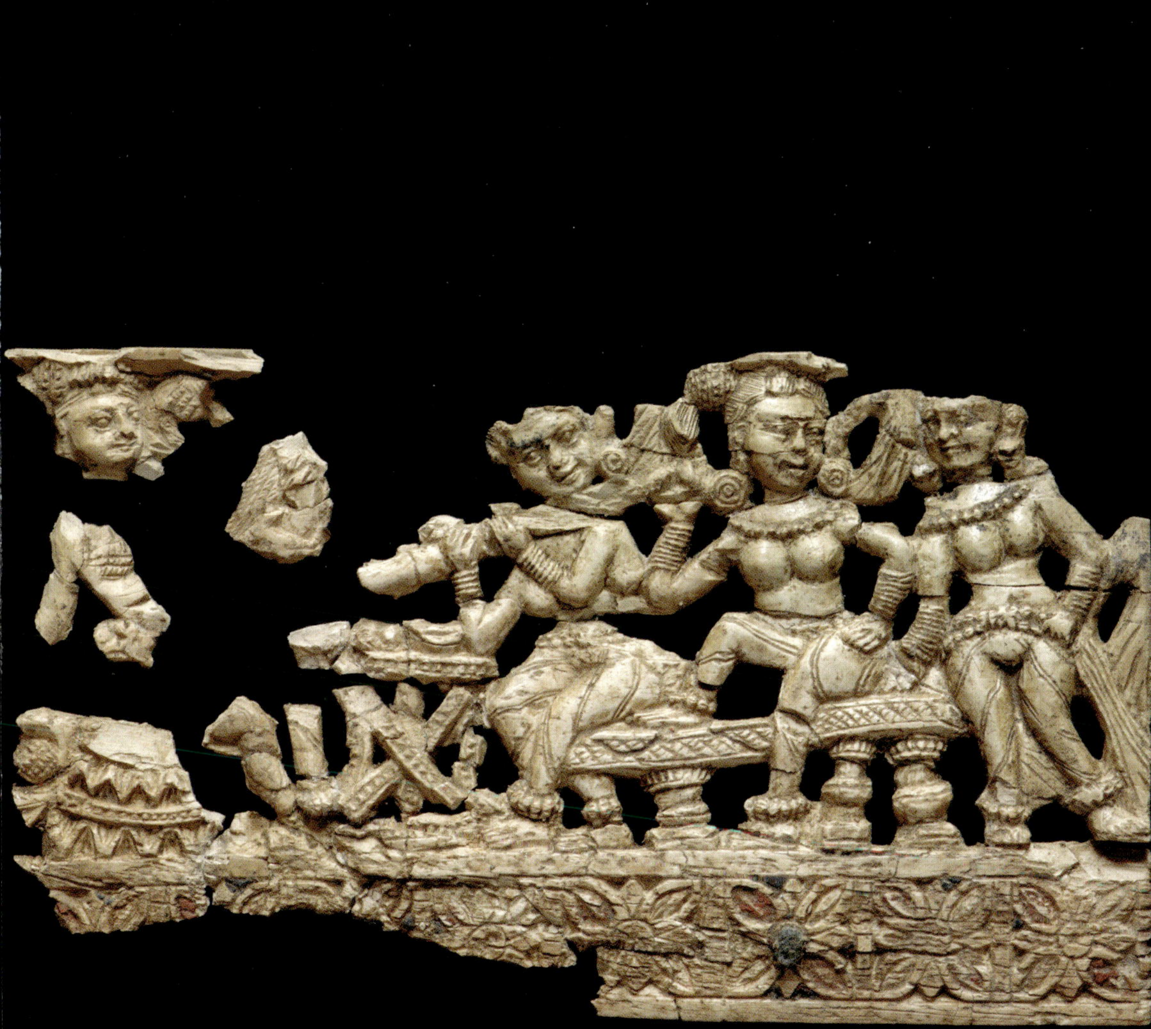

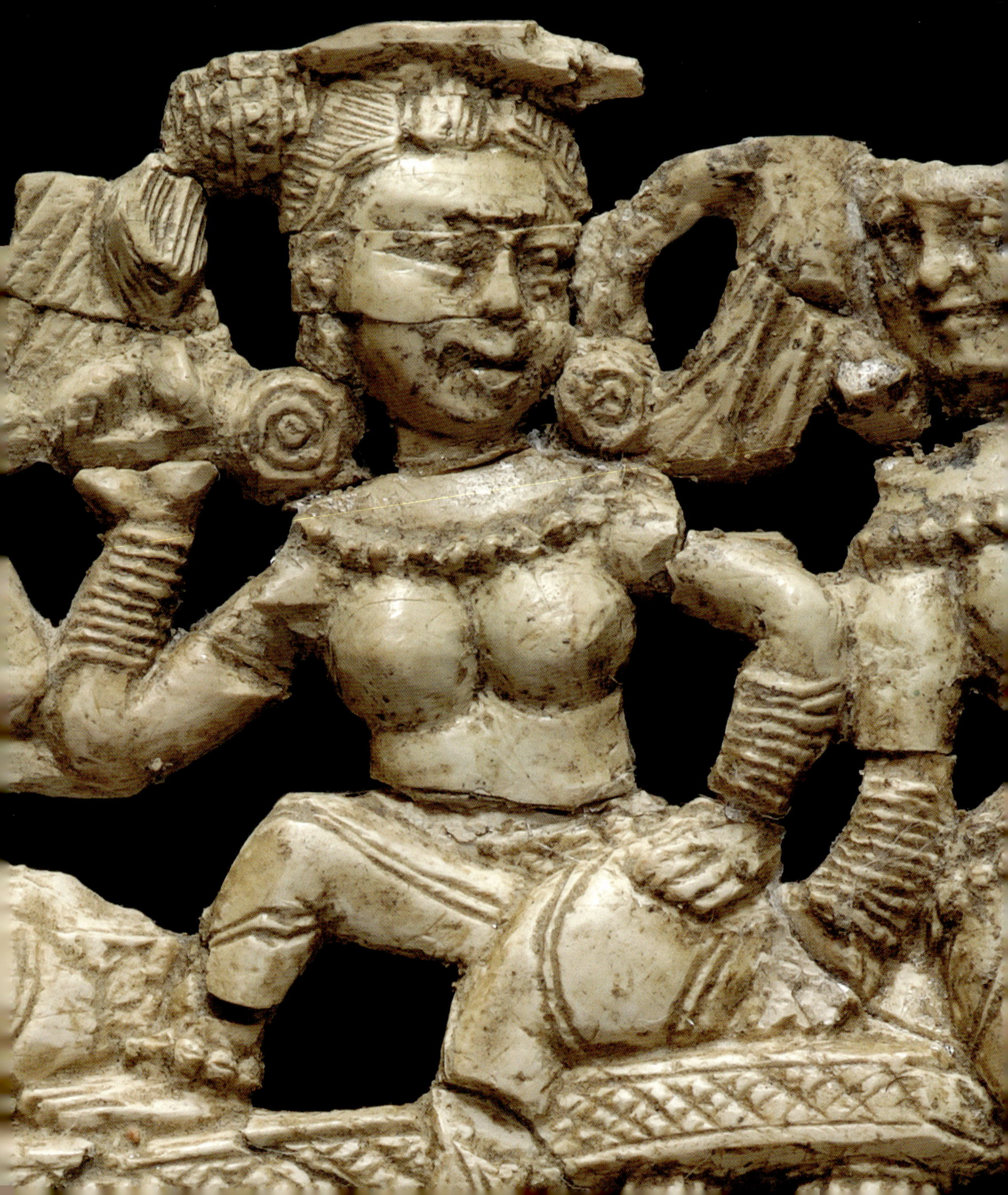

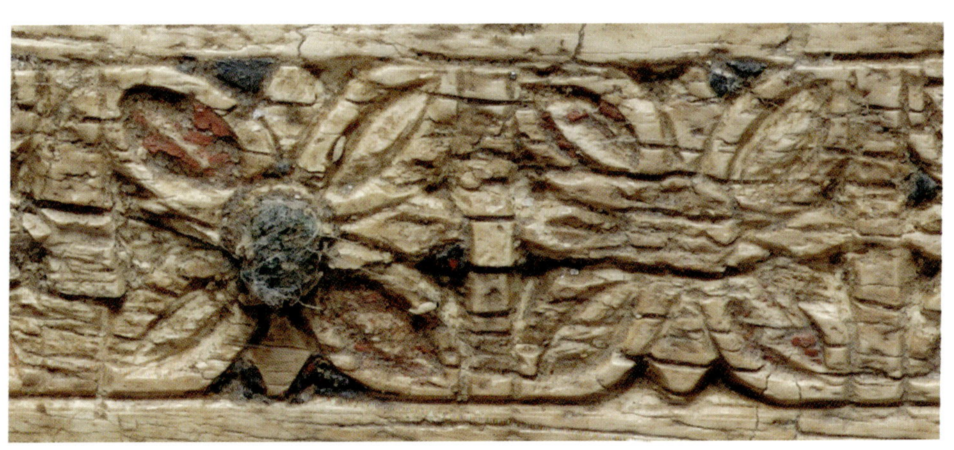

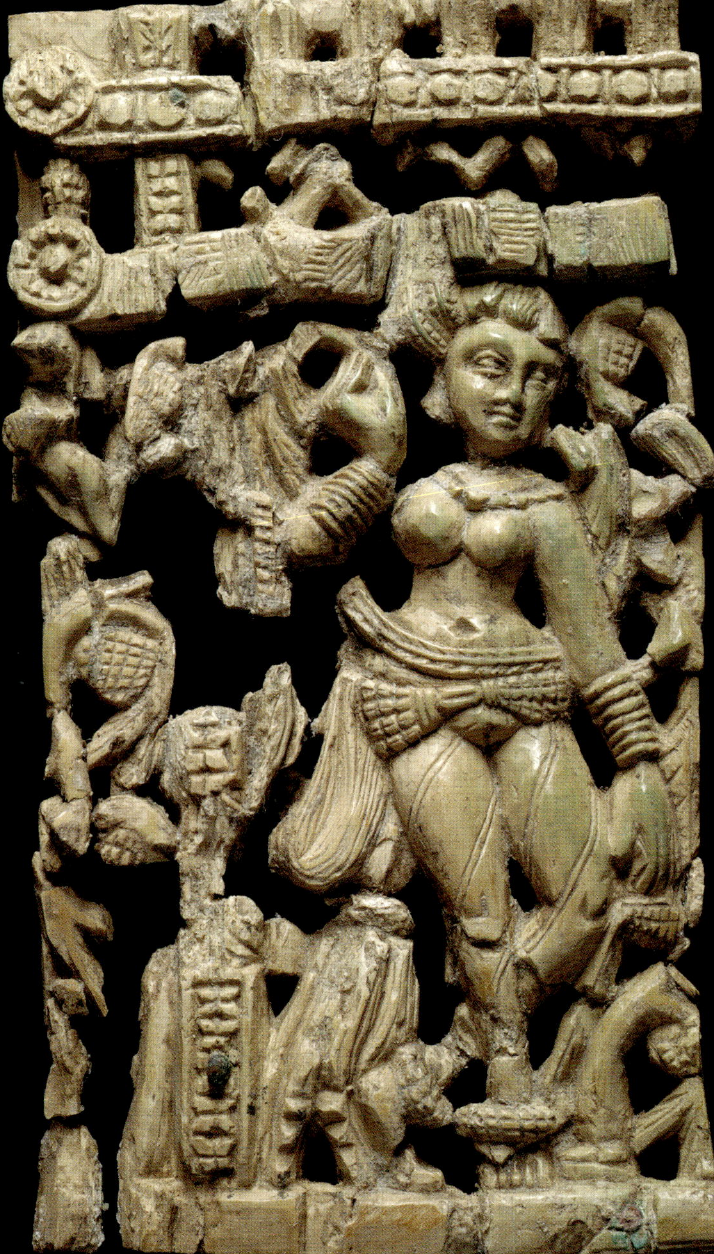

18 *Woman beneath a gateway*

H 13.6 × W 7.5 × Th 0.8 cm
Room 13, Chair 1 or 4
K.p.Beg.583.323; K.M. inv. no. 58–1–42
Hackin 1954: 223–4, fig. 66, no. 196; Tissot 2006: 240

Openwork ivory inlay panel showing a topless woman clutching a branch of the *ashoka* tree and wearing a necklace, multiple bangles on each forearm, prominent decorative anklets and a heavy multiple-strand beaded hip girdle over a lower garment. The latter is rendered with pairs of diagonal incised lines, perhaps intended to show folds but more likely to represent decorative stripes. The identification of the figures as topless has been challenged, as some of the individuals shown on later cave paintings at Ajantā are actually wearing transparent garments. The inlay was secured with copper alloy rivets measuring 0.1–0.2 cm across and passed through the gate uprights, the corner of the upper architrave and the plain border at the bottom. The surface of the inlay is partly stained green through accidental contact with copper during burial.

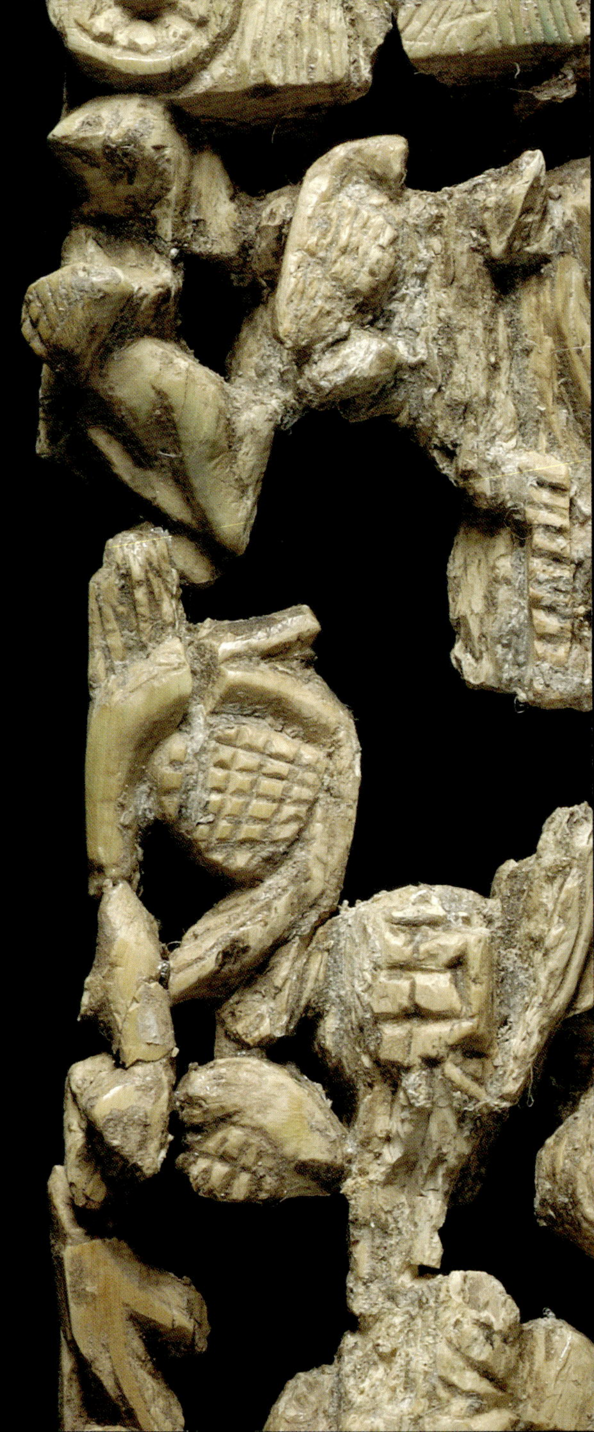

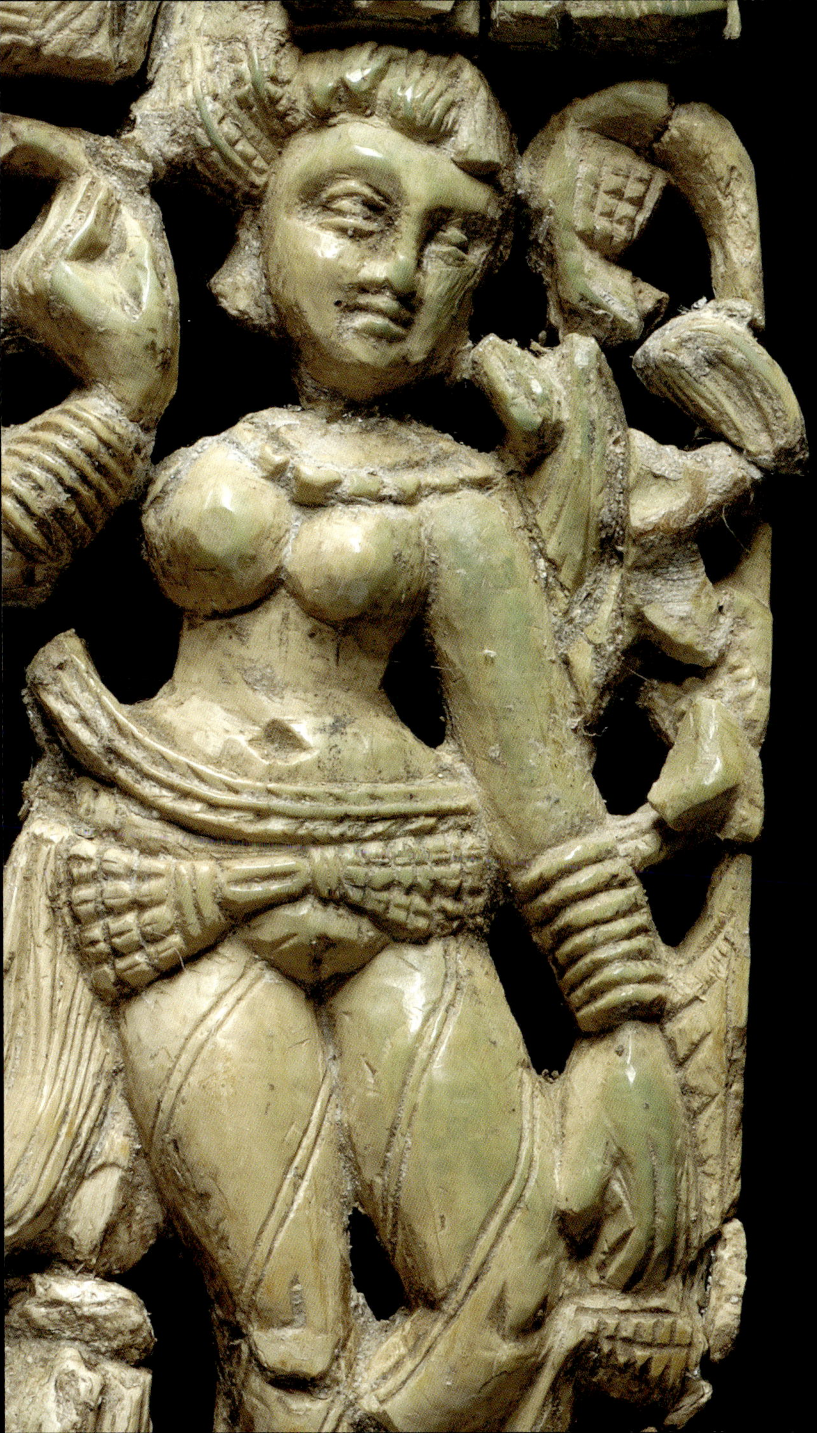

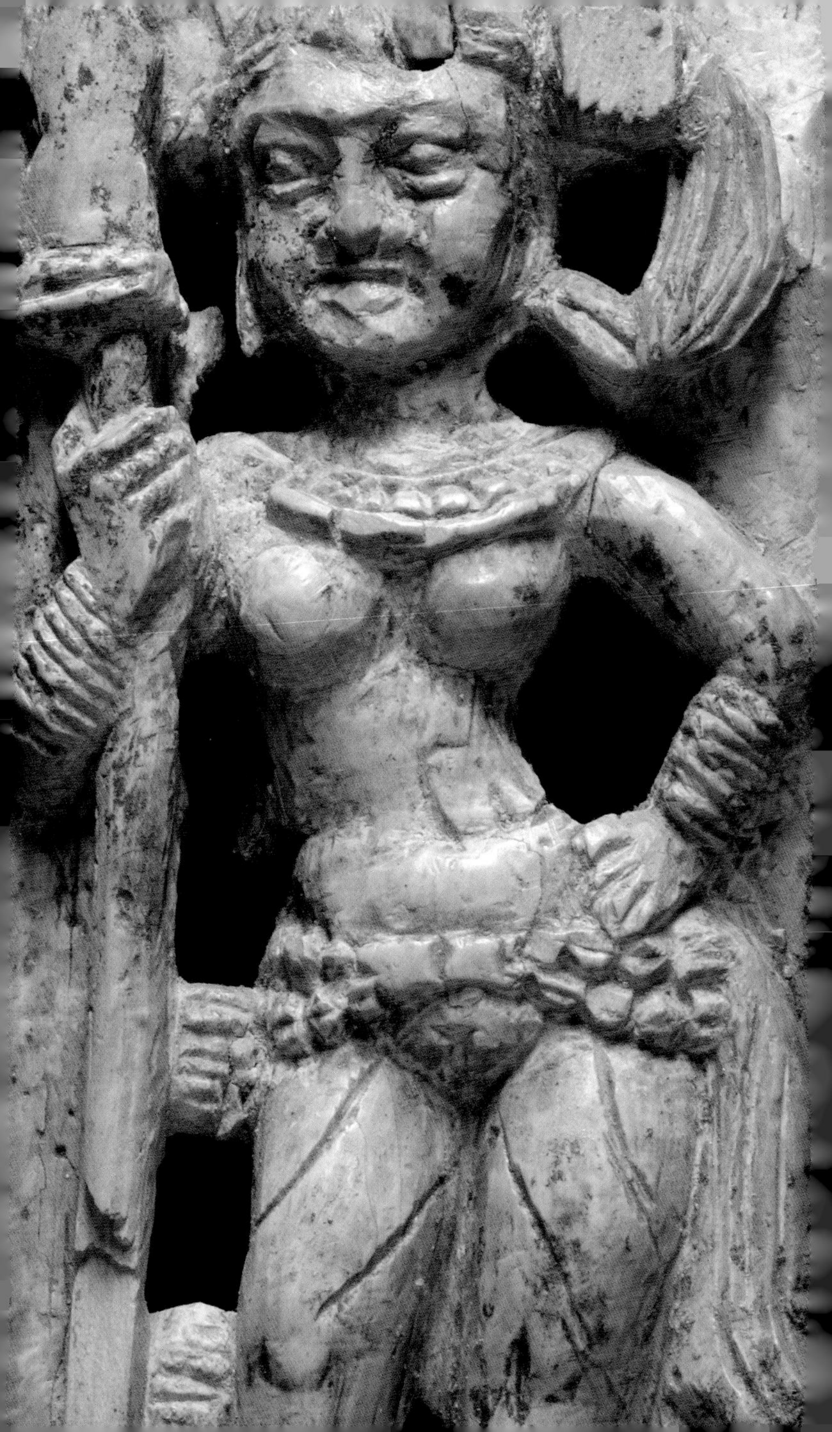

H 8.6 × W 3.3 × Th 1.1 cm
Room 13, plaque
K.p.Beg.607.347; K.M. inv. no. 58–1–76
Hackin 1954: 238–9, fig. 12, no. 211c; Tissot 2006: 249

Openwork ivory panel showing a woman carved in identical style to **18**, holding a spear in her right hand. This was originally secured with a pair of small copper alloy rivets, 0.2 cm across at the head; one was passed through the inlay above the top of the head (but is now missing) and the second through the lower frame between the feet.

The inlay was part of a much larger composition with a central panel showing two women feeding ducks under a tree, framed by pilasters supporting recumbent bull capitals, a row of elephants on the pediment and a pair of spear-holding women at the bottom right and left. These women are *dvarapali* (gate guardians).

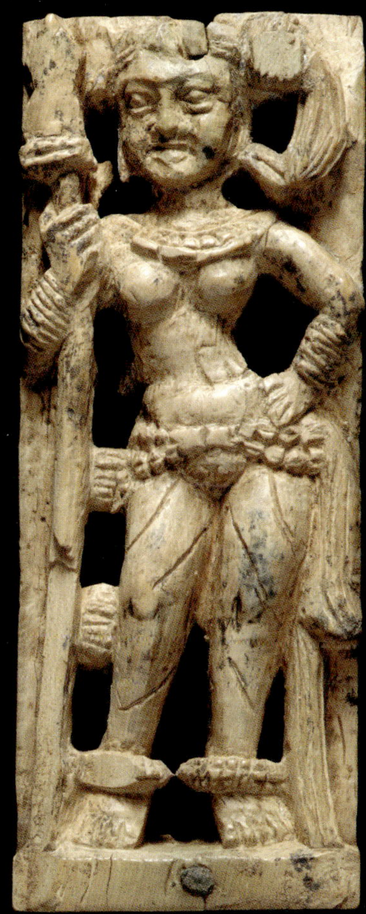

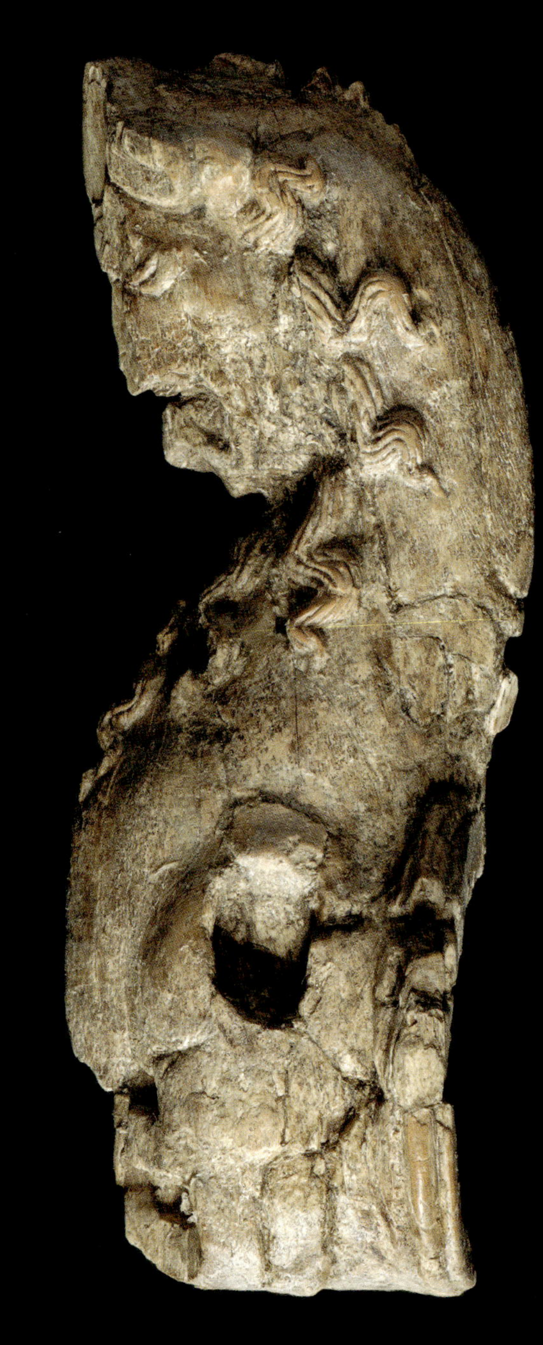

20 *Carved furniture element*

H 12.6 × W 4 × Th 3.2 cm
Previously unpublished

Carved from bone, this shows a head and curving
neck with flowing locks of hair framing the
badly preserved face. There is a large dowel hole
at the back for attachment to another piece of
the furniture.

Conclusion

by Omara Khan Massoudi, Director of the National Museum of Afghanistan

OVER the decades following the outbreak of war in Afghanistan in 1979, the contents of the National Museum were packed, unpacked and moved several times, and in May 1993 the upper part of the building was destroyed by shelling. During this period of confusion some of our objects were mislaid. The fate of these exquisite ivory inlays remained uncertain and we feared them to be lost forever.

They have been identified and recently acquired on behalf of the National Museum of Afghanistan and we are very grateful to all those concerned who have been responsible for this very generous act. This serves to remind the world of the importance of safeguarding cultural heritage and preserving the highest level of ethics. We also hope that this will inspire others to continue in this way to work with us for a better understanding of the rich culture of Afghanistan.

It is wonderful to be able to show these pieces here in London at the British Museum as part of our exhibition, *Afghanistan: Crossroads of the Ancient World*. We are grateful that this has also created an opportunity for them to be properly conserved so that they are now fit for exhibition and future display in the National Museum in Kabul.

Bibliography and further reading

Casson, L., 1989. *The Periplus Maris Erythraei*, Princeton: Princeton University Press.

Cutler, A., 1985. *The Craft of Ivory: Sources, Techniques, and Uses in the Mediterranean World (A.D. 100–1400)*, Washington, DC: Dumbarton Oaks.

Dwivedi, V.P., 1976. *Indian Ivories (A Survey of Indian Ivory and Bone Carvings from the Earliest to the Modern Times)*, New Delhi: Agam.

Errington, E. and Sarkhosh Curtis, V., eds, 2007. *From Persepolis to the Punjab. Exploring Ancient Iran, Afghanistan and Pakistan*, London: British Museum Press.

Gill, S., 2001. 'Procédés narratives dans les ivories de Begram', *Topoi* 11, 515–35.

Hackin, J., 1939. *Recherches archéologiques à Begram: Chantier no. 2, 1937*, Paris: Délégation Archéologique Française en Afghanistan, Mémoire IX.

__________, 1954. *Nouvelles recherches archéologiques à Begram, ancient Kâpicî*, Paris: Délégation Archéologique Française en Afghanistan, Mémoire XI.

Hiebert, F. and Cambon, P., eds, 2011. *Afghanistan. Hidden Treasures from the National Museum, Kabul*, London: British Museum Press (revised edn).

MacGregor, A., 1985. *Bone, Antler, Ivory & Horn. The Technology of Skeletal Materials Since the Roman Period*, London and Sydney: Croom Helm.

Mallowan, M.E.L., 1966. *Nimrud and its Remains*, London: Collins.

Mehendale, S., 1997. Begram: New Perspectives on the Ivory and Bone Carvings. PhD dissertation, University of California, Berkeley, http://www.ecai.org/begramweb/.

__________, 2001. 'The Begram ivory and bone carvings: some observations on provenance and chronology', *Topoi* 11, 485–514.

Nehru, L., 2004. 'A fresh look at the bone and ivory carvings from Begram', *Silk Road Art & Archaeology* 10, 97–150.

Rosen Stone, E., 2008. 'Some Begram ivories and the South Indian narrative tradition: new evidence', *Journal of Inner Asian Art & Archaeology* 3/3, 45–59.

Seland, E.H., 2010. *Ports and Political Power in the Periplus: Complex Societies and Maritime Trade on the Indian Ocean in the First Century AD*, Oxford: Archaeopress.

Tissot, F., 2006. *Catalogue of the National Museum of Afghanistan 1931–1985*, Paris: UNESCO.

Whitehouse, D., 1989. 'Begram, the *Periplus* and Gandharan art', *Journal of Roman Archaeology* 2, 93–100.

__________, 2001. 'Begram: the glass', *Topoi* 11, 437–49.

Whitteridge, G., 1986. *Charles Masson of Afghanistan. Explorer, Archaeologist, Numismatist and Intelligence Agent*, Warminster: Aris & Phillips.

Acknowledgements

WE are indebted to all concerned who have been involved in the recovery of these pieces. The conservation and scientific research was carried out in the British Museum within an extremely short period of time and we are very grateful to David Saunders, Kenneth Uprichard and Catherine Higgitt for their full support, and to the exhibition sponsor Bank of America Merrill Lynch for helping make this possible. The conservation was carried out by Clare Ward and Barbara Wills. The scientific research was carried out by Catherine Higgitt, Janet Ambers, Emma Passmore, Giovanni Verri and Caroline Cartwright. The pieces were catalogued and the accompanying text written by St John Simpson with contributions by all of the above.

Illustration acknowledgements

All object photographs are copyright the National Museum of Afghanistan and reproduced here with permission. Other illustrations: Warwick Ball (p. 10, top left), Délégation Archéologique Française en Iran (pp. 9, top, bottom, 22, 28, 37), Google Earth (p. 10, bottom left), National Geographic Society (pp. 10, bottom right, 11–13), National Museum of Afghanistan (cover, pp. 5–6, 18–21, 31–4, 38, 40, 42, 45, 46, 48–50, 52–6, 59–60, 62, 64, 67–9, 71–3, 75–7, 79–84, 86–90).